The Handbook for Beach Strollers from Maine to Cape Hatteras

The Handbook for Beach Strollers from Maine to Cape Hatteras

Donald J. Zinn
Professor Emeritus of Zoology, University of Rhode Island
Illustrated by Richard C. Grosvenor

The Globe Pequot Press

For Eleanor

Alles ist aus dem Wasser entsprungen!!
Alles wird durch das Wasser erhalten!
Ocean gönn' uns dein ewiges Walten.

Faust II by Johann Wolfgang von Goethe

"Read Nature not books. If you study Nature in
books, when you go out-of-doors you cannot find her."

Louis Agassiz

The original edition of *The Beach Strollers Handbook* was made up of 35 short articles, written as contributions to *Maritimes,* the quarterly publication of the University of Rhode Island's Graduate School of Oceanography. It was published in book form as Marine Bulletin Number 12 by the University of Rhode Island in 1973.

Contents

5   Introduction by Alfred L. Hawkes

7   Exploring the Sandy Beach at Low Tide

10   The Rich Animal and Plant Life in "The Spaces in Between"

12   The Sponge—An Ancient but Efficient Animal

16   Yes, there are Corals in North Atlantic Waters

18   Jellyfish—Largely Water and Worldwide in Distribution

21   The Jellyfish That Isn't

24   Bait for Your Hooks

27   A Can of Sea Worms

30   Little Known Vermiform Denizens of the Tidelands

33   New England Marine Flatworms

35   Barnacles—The Clinging Crustaceans

39   *Callinectes sapidus*, Favorite Target of *Homo sapiens*

41   The Crab That Solved the Housing Problem

44   And other Crabs

52   Freshwater Shellfish Delicacy

53   Lobster Lore, The American Lobster

56   The Native Shrimp

60   The Horseshoe Crab—A Living Fossil

63   Dollars in the Sand

66   The Native Sea Cucumbers

69   The Sea Urchin and its Life

71   Star of the Sea

74   New England's Most Primitive Living Marine Mollusk

77   Jingle Shells, the Beachcomber's Delight

80   A Local Snail That Harbors Bather's Itch

82   It Reminded the Greeks of a Mouse

83   Oysters "R" for Eating

86   The Immigrant Snail

88   The Sharpest Clam of All

91   In Favor of Sea Slugs

93   The Squid—Denizen of the Sea and Delicacy for the Diner

95   Termites of the Sea

97   The Surf Clam, New England's Largest Marine Bivalve

99   The North Atlantic Coast's Largest Edible Snails

102   Queen Quahog

106   Orchestia, The Sand Dancer

110   When the Tide is Out, Dinner is Served

122   References

124   Index

Introduction
Alfred L. Hawkes
Executive Director, Audubon Society of Rhode Island

For at least two generations, the elementary and secondary public schools and most institutions of higher learning have nurtured the myth that through science man can solve all his problems. Most of us over thirty were educated to believe that technology need only have enough attention paid and sufficient homage provided and, through it, man will sooner or later emerge supreme over all physical and biological earthly constraints.

We were led to believe that the best educated man was the technician who knew the most about the least—whose horizons were narrowest but most penetrating—who could speak of his subject only to his researchers and not even to them if he was really the best in his line. Because the fashionable sciences were biochemistry, molecular biology, biophysics, cytology, nuclear physics, physical engineering and similar inward-peering disciplines, whole curricula were revised to allow entire faculties of teacher-researchers (a contradiction in temperaments, it seems to me) to inflict their interests on a generation or more of hapless high school and college students.

For most of us, science—biology in particular—came to mean hour upon hour of deadly lectures on aspects of life which were meaningless without an enthusiasm, an understanding, even a reverence for the commonplace inhabitants of the garden, pond, shore or woods.

For those who, like myself, found unending fascination in living things (as opposed to formalin-soaked corpses), biology was one of the great disappointments. Learning to recognize life in the field was frowned on as "outdated." "It has all been done before," we were told. The pleasure of knowing where and how to find a particular animal or plant, understanding its behavioral characteristics, its food or its sex life, was looked on as frivolous since it made no contribution to extending the bounds of total knowledge. To be a respectable biologist, one had to be "research oriented." The animal itself, its community and its relationship to that community were not worthy of the attention of a biologist.

At the time, we wished we could find another kind of professor: one to whom the living thing was superior to the pickled cadaver, to whom life bore some relation to living; one who saw a living object as the four-dimensional product of a two-billion-year experience, an object that had a direct bearing on man's existence and was directly affected by sharing a planet with him. We couldn't have expressed it that way, and we needed someone who could. We were looking for someone who today would be called an ecologist.

Donald J. Zinn is that kind of scientist. An internationally known zoologist and former chairman of the Department of Zoology at the University of Rhode Island, to which he came as instructor in 1946, Don Zinn has known for years that there is much to life and living that no scientist can measure or understand. He finds fascination in the unknown and satisfaction in putting the known into context in the web that consists of man, animal, plant and environment. Like many of the earlier bio-philosophers, he communicates to his audience that other living things are at least as interesting as people, and occasionally of far more significance to the planet as a whole. It is this conviction that made him a tireless participant in conservation efforts, long before they became fashionable, climaxing his service with three terms as president of the National Wildlife Federation. A lesser, but for his friends and readers almost equally rewarding passion, has been his lifelong pursuit of delicious ways to cook and eat some of the creatures he studies. He is known as a "bio-gourmet" of considerable imagination, and he shares much of his culinary knowledge in this book.

If you are one of those who is aware of the pleasures of beachcombing, of gathering your own mess of clams to steam in a bucket, of climbing a hill for the wind and the view, of collecting leaves for pressing, or fishing without caring what or even if success results, if you believe that knowledge and understanding are worthwhile ends in themselves, you will surely enjoy this book.

Exploring the Sandy Beach at Low Tide

At nearly any time of the year, the sandy Atlantic shores lining our coast from Maine to Cape Hatteras can provide the pleasurable anticipation of discovery of "treasures" of many origins, shapes and compositions.

Most of the sands on these seashores were brought by currents and tides from the Continental Shelf and deposited on the beach by waves; some came from the weathering of rocks along the coastal regions by wind, waves and rain, and the rest were transported by rivers and estuaries and then deposited along the shore by prevailing coastal currents. Originally, a large part of this sand had a glacial origin, being deposited with the melting of glacial ice and the formation of outwash plains (the broad flood plains of glacial meltwater streams—often underlain by sand and gravel). Every storm, and indeed every tide, sifts and re-sorts the sand making it relatively easy for even the casual observer to see a continuing reworking and remaking of the beach. The constant motion grinds the sediments, making the sand particles smaller, and scattering them in accordance with their new mass, the small lighter particles being transported farther than the larger, heavier particles. Thus the higher parts of the beach ordinarily tend to have a deeper layer of fine sand than the stretch along the water line.

Our beach sands consist mainly of crushed quartz of various colors interspersed with a number of minerals such as biotite, semi-precious gems like garnets, as well as inclusions of particles of the shells of snails and bivalves. A random sample of beach sand spread under the low power of a compound microscope reveals a granular landscape of varying and sometimes brilliant color and unique angular and rounded shapes, together with bits and pieces of detritus from many sources.

For those who like to collect varicolored and multishaped pebbles and cobbles, there are both exposed beds and secluded pockets of often beautifully smoothed cabochons or egg-shaped chunks of quartz, feldspars, granites, gneisses, sandstones, phyllites, graphites, argillites, sericites, and conglomerates. Occasionally, a piece of coal or brick, now well rounded, can be found. A fortunate collector may even find one of the small, beautifully rounded greenish "moonstones." "Sea glass," frosted, odd-shaped bits of glass worn by the sea into translucent reds, browns, blues, purples, greens and yellows, is also there for the observant beachcomber.

Often the most commonly encountered materials are rows of live, dying or dead seaweeds along the upper part of the beach, each row left behind at the level of high water. A single line of seaweed represents the last spring tide; the lower of several rows indicates both the height of the last high tide, and the difference in height of the two tides. The rows of seaweed are usually composed of species found immediately offshore, although occasionally there may be flora mixed in that has been floating and drifting offshore for a long time, such as sargassum. Kinds of seaweeds ordinarily included in tide rows along Atlantic beaches in addition to the unique marine seed plant, eelgrass, are the algae: Irish moss, palmated kelp, laminaria, rock weeds, bladder wrack, sea-lettuce, sponge seaweed, devil's-apron and dulse. All manner of living and dead organisms as well as inanimate material may be wrapped in the seaweeds as they are rolled up the slope of the beach in tidal waters.

Insects are uncommon in all marine habitats. However, in the tide rows of seaweed live several kinds of biting flies among which are the greenheaded flies; the eelgrass flies; the true seaweed flies whose larvae have been recorded preying on the eggs of a marine fish; and the chersodromid flies that run about because of their drastically reduced wings. If the rotting seaweed is kicked or otherwise disturbed, a large number of small jumping animals pop out. These are crustaceans called sand-fleas or beach-hoppers, which feed on the seaweed and burrow in the sand.

On some beaches there may be an abundance of thin, sand-colored collars, two or three inches high. These are the egg masses of the moon snail whose eggs are embedded in jelly in the sand collars. Other odd looking structures are the empty black rectangular cases with a curled or horn-shapped extension at each corner. These are the egg purses or egg cases of the common skate which have become detached from their subtidal anchorage and washed onto the beach. Very striking are the spirally coiled strings of parchment-like discs, about two feet long, each disc containing wedge-shaped compartments with many eggs. These clusters of discs are the egg cases of the large whelks; if they are picked up and gently shaken, the shells of the young, probably dead, whelks rattle interestingly.

Sometimes the perfect shells of molted crabs, cast during growth, are carried onto the beach by the tide. It is often easy to identify the kind and sex of the crab from which undamaged shells came. Of course, parts of dead crabs and other invertebrate animals are often scattered about, death having occurred from any one of a variety of natural causes. Driftwood logs and old crates are commonplace on the beach. Careful searching along the outside of this wood may reveal acorn or ivory barnacles, periwinkles or other snails, and sometimes bits of kelp that may have strands of lace-like hydroids growing on it, or be encrusted with the rounded, sometimes strikingly colored colonies of ectoprocts or moss animals. The driftwood may also contain the calcium-carbonate-lined burrows of bivalve shipworms, or the smaller-bored termite-like tubes of the burrowing crustaceans known as gribbles. It is said that no matter how riddled with shipworms a piece of driftwood may be, its galleries never join or interfere with each other. On some wood, there may even be the twisting calcified white tubes that at one time housed polychaete annelids, relatives of the common sand-dwelling clam worm.

All sizes of casts (molts) of horseshoe crab skeletons may be found on occasion. These casts are often in such good condition, in such life-like positions that a neophyte must examine them closely to find out wether they are alive. Probably the largest amount of recognizable organic inanimate material along the beach derives from the shells of pelecypods (bivalves) and gastropods (snails). Mollusk shells are found in all stages of fracture and decay: color may be bleached by the sun, chips and breakage are common, edges may be dulled by rolling in the surf and by abrasion. These factors often make positive identification difficult. Usually the best collecting in terms of variety of species is accomplished directly after an onshore storm.

Other items that may be found on occasion are a variety of sponges including the fairly common, light brown, digitate deadman's fingers; the floating and attached zooids (including the strings of stinging cells) of the coelenterate siphonophore, the Portuguese man-of-war (usually late August); the skeleton of the common stony coral which forms masses rarely larger than one's fist: large jellyfish such as the ubiquitous moonjelly, the giant reddish arctic jellyfish, the frilled jellyfish and sometimes the stalked jellyfish. The tests of shells of such echinoderms (spiny-skinned animals) as the round, domeshaped pentamerous sea urchin are also found; and the thickly gelatinous, massive, compound, translucent gray, tough sea squirt (protochordate), which because it suggests salt pork in color and consistency is known as sea pork. Often a person collecting sea pork for the first time is sure that he has suddenly made it rich by finding a supply of ambergris!

The Rich Animal and Plant Life
in "The Spaces in Between"

If summer occupants of beach cottages and other oceanside accommodations, surfers, beachcombers, fishermen, swimmers, sunbathers and sundry additional categories of itinerant thalassopsammophiles (beach lovers) will take the necessary additional small amount of time and effort, they may observe an exciting and virtually newly-discovered microfauna and microflora living on and between the grains of sand beneath their feet. These microscopic animals and plants live in great variety and in tremendous numbers in the upper layers of Atlantic beaches. They may be found also in similarly large numbers in subtidal sand under water to a depth of several meters.

The easiest way to collect these organisms is to take a small shovelful of sand about halfway between the tide lines and put it in a large pail with enough sea water to cover it to a depth of about two inches. The sample of sand should extend from the surface to a depth of three or four inches. After the sand is kneaded for two or three minues by hand, the excess wash water is poured into a small glass where it may be examined with a strong hand lens. The amazingly active, interstitial (in the space between) fauna and flora may now readily be seen except for some of the very smallest forms which are better observed with a stereo or dissecting microscope.

Another way to collect the interstitial fauna is to dig into the beach at the half tide line until the water table is reached. A sufficiently large hole is made so that the water may be swished quite thoroughly with hands or with a small tropical fish dip net, or a similar type of net frame covered at home with the finest marquisette. If the sand and water are mixed manually a small glass jar can be used to scoop up the sand water; if a net is used it may be inverted and dipped (washed) into a similar small glass containing clear sea water.

The interstitial fauna and flora live in sand and sandy sediments in seas, lakes, rivers, springs and other bodies of salt, brackish and fresh waters. These animals and plants may also be found where there are similar sandy areas bordering such waters, providing these soils are constantly damp. The biologist has given these organisms the collective name, psammon; the fresh and brackish water forms are called mesopsammon, while the marine speices are known as thalassopsammon.

Investigations of the thalassopsammon have been more numerous because the interstitial fauna has attained its most varied development in marine sediments. Most of the large categories of invertebrates are represented in the marine sand microfauna, some groups in great variety, and many species display a structure of amazing interest; some represent unique types of organization.

The morphological adaptations of both microflora and microfauna to their extraordinary habitat are often little less than fantastic. The animals are obliged to squeeze between the sand grains and glide over the surfaces of adjacent sediment particles sometimes on the surface films of water and at other times through capillary water. At the same time, they must withstand the rigors of tides, waves and storms. In general, natural selection has left them with elognated and usually flattened or threadlike bodies, lack of pigmentation, remarkably developed organs of adhesion, various kinds of sensory bristles, and a reduction in gonads especially in the females.

The marine interstitial fauna is a population of often bizarre organisms in an equally unique environment about which the barest details are known at the present time. It is a fascinating group biologically presenting challenges to the botanist, zoologist and the geologist to discover its origins, relationships, organization and perhaps eventually its applications to the business of man.

The Sponge—An Ancient but Efficient Animal

Among the most primitive organisms along Atlantic shores are a large group of creatures whose animal nature was not fully recognized by all biologists until a little more than a hundred years ago. The question was, "Since sponges neither move about nor, apparently, respond rapidly to direct stimuli from their environment, how can they capture food?" Then an imaginative investigator thought of suspending tiny particles in the water near the sponge, and saw these bits of particulate matter slowly disappear. Further investigation revealed jets of water issuing from holes at the tops of the animals, and closer inspection showed that water was constantly entering through microscopic pores that penetrate the entire surface of the animals. This discovery eventually led to the now well-substantiated observation that sponges act like animated filters, feeding on the great variety of microscopic fauna and flora as well as on the fine bits of detritus that ordinarily occur in the waters surrounding them. It also became the basis for the name given the phylum to which all sponges belong, Porifera, or pore-bearing animals. It is for this reason as well, that sponges cannot live out of water; indeed, their whole existence depends on a continual flow of clean aerated water passing through their bodies.

Sponges are thought to have evolved in the Precambrian period, more than 600 million years ago. They are considered the most primitive of the many-celled animals: they have neither true tissues nor organs, their cells exhibit a large degree of independence, all members of the phylum are sessile, or attached to the substrate, and display little detectable movement. Although the mists of time have made the origin of sponges uncertain, most zoologists feel that sponges diverged early from the main line of evolution and have given rise to no other groups of animals. In other words, in all probability they are what properly may be called a dead-end phylum.

Sponges are usually found attached to pilings, shells, rocks and other hard substrates, from the intertidal areas and salt ponds to the depths of bays and sounds.

In some areas, almost every rock bears encrusting sponges on its lower surface, and the submerged parts of pilings, especially those not treated with preservative, support many of the smaller sponges. In areas of Narragansett Bay, for example, where oysters still pave parts of the bottom, the boring sponge has invaded a majority of their shells, making them brittle and useless commercially, and often killing the oysters. The more massive and squatter types like the so-called elephant dung sponge, are often found on mud-shell bottoms in the Bay. Still other kinds, for example, the red sponge, are flat and encrusting when they settle on substrates in shallow and turbulent waters, but are more massive and branching in deeper and less disturbed areas. Very often the dead man's finger sponge that grows just offshore, is thrown up on ocean beaches.

At last count, there were 16 species of sponges native to the salt waters of Rhode Island alone. These may be divided into eight genera. *Leucosolenia* are the minute, simply structured, nearly white sponges composed of branching cylindrical tubes that are often found on pilings; *Scypha* are light tan, urn- or

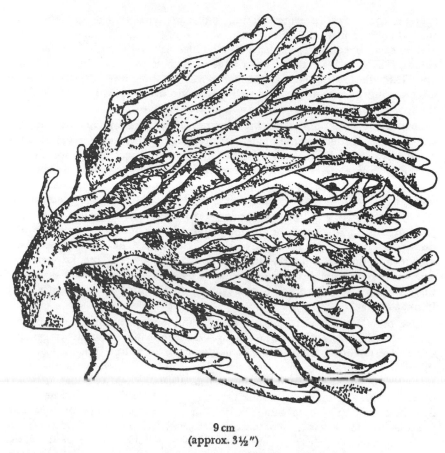

9 cm
(approx. 3½")

Microciona prolifera—The Red Sponge. This common sponge incrusts on shallow, hard substrata but develops into large clusters of finger-like lobes in deeper water.

vase-shaped, and occur singly or in clusters on pilings; *Cliona* is the brilliant sulfur-yellow boring sponge, which is nipple-shaped when removed from its shell substrate. *Haliclona* or dead man's fingers is yellowish tan to gold, encrusted or branched into rounded or flattened fingers rising from a narrow stalk. *Halichondria* or bread-crumb sponge, is orange-yellow to greenish, encrusted and provided with numerous low, upright tubules, each ending in an opening. *Microciona* is a brilliant red to orange-brown sponge, with finger-like projections, found both in and off shore. *Suberites*, the elephant dung sponge is yellow to yellowish gray, shaped in low compact mounds and found off shore. *Mycale* varies in color from yellow-ochre to slate gray and often is found on wharf pilings.

Because sponges vary in form from absolute asymmetry to handsome symmetry, and because they are thought to be so very primitive in structure and function, the question as to exactly what constitutes an individual sponge has often been raised. In the cases of sponges with very definite form like *Scypha*, the vase sponge, or the large sheepswool sponges used for washing cars, the whole sponge is considered an individual. However, in the low encrusting sponges, the answer is more difficult, and here some sponge specialists consider the entire mass as an individual, while other sponge biologists claim that each oscular opening represents an individual and that the whole mass is a colony. The oscula are round holes large enough to be seen with the unaided eye. Through the oscula, water is constantly escaping into the environment after passing through the sponge wall and being involved within the tissues of the sponge walls in both respiration and nutrition.

One of the more important characteristics of sponges for both the biologist and the animal itself are the numerous interlocking spicules or crystalline rods, made of calcium carbonate or of a silicon compound secreted by special cells of the middle tissue layer called scleroblasts. Spicules compose the delicate scaffolding that is the internal skeleton of the animals. In some warm-water sponges, a tough interwoven fabric of horny material takes the place of the crystalline spicules, and in still other deep-sea glass sponges, the silicious spicules join together in what must be the most unusual and one of the most architecturally beautiful skeletons in the animal kingdom. The oldfashioned bath sponge is nothing but the skeleton of a horny sponge! The infinite variety of sizes, shapes and combinations of spicules provides a most important diagnostic characteristic for zoologists who endeavor to distinguish one species of sponge from another.

Like other animals that are sessile and cannot move around, sponges have motile larvae. Nearly all marine sponges are hermaphrodites with eggs and sperm developing at different times in the same organism. The eggs are fertilized inside the sponge and grow there into minute ciliated larvae that eventually go through the osculum into the surrounding water. After a varying period of planktonic life they settle and become fixed on a hard substrate, metamorphose and grow into adults. Many of our local sponges, *Scypha* and *Leucosolenia* for instance, reproduce equally well by budding. Sometimes the buds separate, but when this does not happen, the buds serve to make the colony larger and more massive. The regenerative power of sponges is amazing. Some years ago, the zoologist H. V. Wilson, squeezed a live red sponge, *Microciona*, through a piece of silk into filtered seawater and within weeks the various dissociated cells had come together and developed into a complete sponge. Although a majority of the smaller New England sponges probably live for a year or less, some of the larger, deep water forms may last five or six years.

As might well be imagined, the calcareous and silicious spicules of sponges, together with their sometimes disagreeable odor and noxious chemicals, make them virtually impervious to predation. In the New England area, their only known enemies are certain sea slugs (nudibranchs) that feed on them. On the other hand, the many structural cavities especially in the larger forms, provide shelter and sometimes food for a great variety of small crustaceans, worms, echinoderms and mollusks that, together with their sponge home, compose a unique and interesting community. Certain small crabs live commensally with sponges, using them for both protection and camouflage. One genus of crab, *Dromia*, cuts and places a small piece of sponge on its back and holds it in place with its last pair of legs while it strides about. Gradually the sponge grows over the back, covering it and thus disguising the crab. Another kind of crab grows *Suberites* on its shell; the *Suberites* eventually dissolve the shell, and the hermit crab occupies a capacious cavity within the sponge! Another kind of

14

association, symbiosis (in which host and guest both derive benefit) is formed between *Halichondria* and certain filamentous green algae. In general, symbiotic plants play an important part in the excretory processes of the sponge host by utilizing the wastes of the host in their own metabolism. In turn, the oxygen they release is used by the sponge in respiration. The economic uses of sponges are restricted to their employment as experimental animals by biologists and to the trade between beachcombers and novelty shops.

Yes, there are Corals in North Atlantic Waters

Many Southern New Englanders are greatly surprised to learn they have a coral skeleton in the collection they have made while beachcombing along one of the long sloping beaches that line the shores of Massachusetts, Rhode Island and Eastern Connecticut, because it is thought commonly that all corals are found in the warmer southern waters. To a certain extent this is true: the majority of corals are reef-forming animals that live mainly in the tropical salt waters of the world, for example, off Southern Asia, Bermuda and in the Caribbean, where the minimum water temperature is about 70° Fahrenheit.

A relatively few species of non-reef-forming corals occurring individually as small colonies live in cold waters at moderate depths as far north as the Arctic Ocean. These are the madrepores or stony corals and it is to this group that *Astrangia danae*, the star coral, belongs. It is the only coral found in these waters. Its distribution extends as far south as Florida.

On stones or shells picked up along the beach, one often finds the encrusted skeletons of star coral colonies. The tiny cup-like depressions or tubular prominences, about one eighth of an inch in diameter were the sites of the individual living coral animals. There are commonly five to thirty individuals in a colony, held together by the calcium deposited by the organisms when they were alive.

If the edges of the cups are rounded, the colony has probably been dead for some time, its borders having been worn away by waves grinding it along the bottom and up onto the beach. However, if the edges are sharp and the details of the skeleton clear, it is a recently dead colony and one that is for this reason more valuable to the collector.

Corals, seafans, seapens and the closely related sea anemones (found on pilings, boulders, submerged logs, stones and shells throughout Atlantic bays and our salt ponds) belong to a still larger group of animals, the coelenterates, that includes in addition, such beasts as jellyfish, the Portuguese man-of-war and hydroids. All are characterized by being (1) radially symmetrical, (2) having one opening into the body and (3) the possession of rather complicated stinging cells (nematocysts).

The coelenterates are generally considered to be quite primitive and among the lowest of the many-celled animals. However, reproductive capacities are peculiarly well developed, some species characteristically exhibiting separate sexes while other species have both sexes in the same individual (hermaphrodites). Sexless or asexual reproduction obtains in many other species.

A further complication is found in a great many forms whose life cycle is curiously divided into a sexual (medusa, the swimming stage) and an asexual (polyp, the sessile stage) part, one part apparently alternating with the other during the life cycle. The star corals are coelenterates in which only the polyp or sessile stage is present.

Living individuals are both beautiful and graceful. The slightly bluish or pinkish transparent polyps extend for about ¼ inch above the opaque calcareous base. The edge of the extended disk bears a circlet of several stubby finger-like tentacles whose tips glisten white with light reflecting from large numbers of papillated batteries of the stinging cells. When a minute crustacean

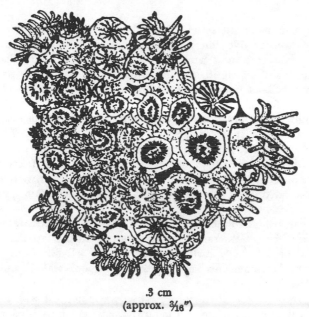

.3 cm
(approx. ³⁄₁₆″)

Astrangia danae—The Star or Northern Coral.

or other microscopic organism touches a tentacle, this living food is subdued by the nematocysts and is thrust toward the central rounded mouth by the folding of the stimulated tentacle acting in concert with its neighbors. In this fashion the prey is quickly engulfed by these basically carnivorous animals. The body wall of the polyps is sufficiently transparent to show the edges of the internal partitions or mesenteries (septa) whose number, distribution and size is important in coral identification.

When polyps die, the soft body parts quickly decompose and are washed away, leaving only the hard calcareous base or skeleton. In these corals this structure made nearly entirely of calcium carbonate is secreted by and is built up around the base of the body in the form of a cup into which the soft parts can retract. The entire polyp grows upward, the hard part by additions to its base, and at a certain stage in its development it divides or buds, eventually attaining the normal stature of the star coral colony. The hard calcareous base is the so-called stony material which gives these corals the designation of stony corals.

A new colony is started when an egg from one coral individual is fertilized by a sperm from another individual, the eventual embryo growing into a microscopic platter-like ciliated organism that becomes a member of the fantastically numerous legions of minute animals suspended in water (zooplankton) for a short time before setting on suitable substratum and metamorphosing into a coral polyp, the progenitor of another colony.

Jellyfish—Largely Water
and Worldwide in Distribution

Ever since man sailed the seven seas, the various sizes and kinds of jellyfish have aroused considerable interest among sailors, fishermen and swimmers. Jellyfish are among the most familiar and common animals in shallow water along the shores and off the islands that dot the coast of New England.

A free living bell—or umbrella-shaped organism, structured of stiff gelatinous material, the jellyfish or medusa either swims (convex shape forward) with more or less rhythmic pulsations using a contractile sheet of muscle near the outer rim, or floats in the water at the mercy of wind, wave or current. The radiating network easily seen through the jelly is made up of canals branching from the stomach, through which food and oxygen-laden sea water is carried.

The bodies of jellyfish are composed of more than 95 percent water combined with minerals and organic material to form a strong and often quite resilient jelly.

These animals belong to the most primitive phylum of true metazoans (many-celled animals), the coelenterates, a name referring to the fact that the central "intestine" is the sole body cavity. In addition to jellyfish, coelenterates, include such animals as anemones, corals, hydroids, seapens, seafans, and the Portuguese man-of-war.

Jellyfish, like other coelenterates, are radially symmetrical with a single central axis from the upper surface to a mouth sometimes surrounded by multiples of four or six variously shaped arms on the base. The parts of the animal are arranged concentrically around this axis.

Very noticeable also are the tentacles, which may be short and stubby or long and slender extensible projections that encircle the rim around the lower end in one or more whorls. Jellyfish have no head, and no centralized nervous system, nor are there definite respiratory, circulatory and excretory systems.

Many species of coelenterates consist of two visually distinct morphological types that alternate in the life cycle of these animals. One type is a sessile or sedentary, essentially tubular, structure, ordinarily attached at one end to a hard substrate by a basal disk or by projecting rootlike branches; the other end terminates in a circular mouth surrounded by a varying number of tentacles. This is called the polyp. It reproduces asexually by budding off from special structures (gonangia). The other morphological type, commonly called jellyfish, is the motile medusa.

The jellyfish or medusa is either male or female and ordinarily has four horseshoe-shaped gonads equidistant in the same plane bearing eggs or sperm. The sexual products are shed, fall into the water, fertilization takes place, and a microscopic, flat, platter-shaped ciliated larva (planula) is produced. After a usually short planktonic existence, the planula settles to a suitable substrate and changes into a polyp type of individual, thus completing the life cycle.

Jellyfish eat large or small prey by snaring and paralyzing passing organisms with the trailing tentacles which then contract, drawing this food to the mouth. The larger jellyfish are capable of capturing relatively large fishes. In any case the prey is ingested whole. Certain jellyfish eat other jellyfish, while smaller jellyfish feed on plankton and organic particles that accidentally become entangled in the mucous of the surface of the bell. Microscopic whiplike flagellae carry this material to the edge of the bell whence it is transferred to the mouth by additional currents along the lower surface of the bell. Sea turtles to some extent, and the giant ocean sunfish, *Mola mola,* to a much greater degree, live by eating the large oceanic jellyfish.

Well over 2,000 years ago, Aristotle in his epic work in natural history, *Historia Animalium,* had a great deal to say about the coelenterates, particularly about the medusae. Interestingly enough, over the years, and even until well past the Renaissance and into the early 19th century, their apparent combination of plant and animal characteristics influenced early biologists toward including them with marine plants. It wasn't until the work first of Ellis, Tremblay and Peyssonel, and later the great Louis Agassiz, that the biology of coelenterates became known. Indeed, G. O. Mackie, a specialist in coelenterate neurophysiology and neuroanatomy, is satisfied that Agassiz was the first person to provide an acceptable description of nerves in a coelenterate. A large number of coelenterates is found as fossils; both relatively complex corals and jellyfish are found in rocks dating back more than 400 million years.

Over the years man has become actively aware of the coelenterates whose nematocysts are capable of inflicting painful stings. Fortunately, in only a few groups of jellyfish are the nematocysts capable of penetrating human skin. In addition to the hydrozoan siphonophores, the major groups of stinging coelenterates belong to a class of large and specialized jellyfish known as the *Scyphozoa* or sea-nettle. One type of particularly dangerous sea-nettle, the sea wasp, is found in the tropical waters of Australia. Less hazardous is *Cyanea capillata,* the so-called "pink jellyfish," the giant or arctic jellyfish of the Atlantic Ocean (known to Sherlock Holmes) whose lens-shaped disk may reach a diameter of eight feet, and whose more than 800 trailing tentacles may extend 200 feet into the water. Ordinarily the *Cyanea* south of Cape Cod and in Narragansett Bay are of smaller size and are relatively harmless, rarely becoming larger than a foot in diameter.

In addition to the Portuguese man-of-war, sometimes found in the fall, and *Cyanea* (to mid-June), other large jellyfish in North Atlantic coastal waters include a number of species of the small hydrozoan and of the microscopic interstitial hydroid medusae; *Gonionemus murbachii,* sometimes in eel grass; *Liriope scutigera,* yellow green in color; *Haliclystus auricula* or stalked jellyfish, a small, variously colored, curiously attached type of medusa that lives as if it were an anemone; *Periphylla hyacinthina,* with a high, narrowly pointed bell; *Pelagia cyanella,* purple-rose to blue, luminescent at night; and *Dactylometra quinquecirrha,* the frilled jellyfish with 40 golden yellow tentacles.

Perhaps the species most often seen washed up on beaches in Southern New England is *Aurelia aurita,* the common and abundant "white sea jelly" or moon jelly with a relatively flattened saucer-shaped disk whose milky white color often contrasts with the prominent pink horseshoe-shaped gonads of the male.

The stinging cells or nematocysts of jellyfish are distributed widely over the surface especially in the region of the mouth and the tentacles, where they may be gathered in warlike clusters of nematocyst batteries. The nematocysts are anchored in underlying tissue by a rootlike structure while the exposed end terminates in a bristle-like trigger. When the trigger is released by mechanical

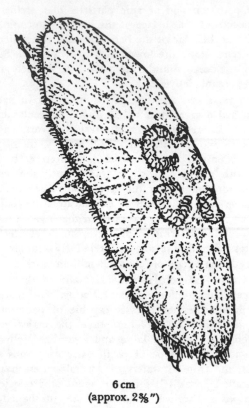

6 cm
(approx. 2⅜")

A side view of *Aurelia aurita*—The White or Moon Jellyfish. The horseshoe-shaped structures are gonads.

or other stimulus (discharge response is independently controlled by each nematocyst), a coiled tube springs from the flask-shaped cell, discharging the contents of the cell-reservoir into the environment or into the object touched. Once released, a nematocyst cannot be used again.

The "sting" of the majority of jellyfish is not perceptible to man. Of course there is a great deal of individual variation from species to species; and thin-skinned, very young, allergic and similarly incapacitated people suffer far more than their opposites. Even in the relatively less dangerous northern waters, most very large jellyfish should be approached with caution: *Cyanea* produces a burning sensation and *Dactylometra* can cause lesions and illness as well. The poisons produced are alkaloidal and may include such compounds as thalassin, congestin and hyprotoxin. It is thought that the more serious manifestations of jellyfish contact result from anaphylactic shock especially in cases where the person may have been stung previously by the same species.

Treatment for jellyfish stings consists of thoroughly washing the affected area of the skin with a harsh soap such as tincture of green soap, followed by the application of calamine, alcohol, vinegar, bluing, witch hazel, bicarbonate of soda paste or other soothing lotion. In more severe cases ice packs should be applied and a physician should be consulted at the earliest possible moment.

The Jellyfish That Isn't

In August and September, swimmers in the coastal waters of Massachusetts, Rhode Island and Connecticut are likely to encounter small walnut-shaped, nearly transparent, delicate, jelly-like, planktonic animals, the so-called comb jellies, sea walnuts or sea gooseberries. These are the ctenophores. They are commonly washed, blown, and driven into windrows and slowly circulating masses against the sides of docks and in the lee of ships at anchor, or against gently sloping subtidal sands. The natural reaction for a swimmer is to think that he is bumping into jellyfish and that he will probably be painfully reminded of these accidental encounters. Of course he would be wrong on both counts; comb jellies belong to a different phylum from jellyfish, Ctenophora rather than Coelenterata, and with one small exception that is not found in these waters, no comb jellies have stinging cells.

Comb jellies live in all of the oceans to depths of more than 10,000 feet and are often found in unimaginably large numbers. The eight rows of characteristic ciliary combs (Greek for comb is ctene, whence the name ctenophore) radiate over the surface of the animal from the upper to the lower pole like the lines of longitude on a globe of the world. The cilia on each comb beat as one, and the eight rows of combs beat synchronously, propelling the animals so slowly and feebly that they are at the mercy of currents and tides. This is the main reason that at times they may be found in swarms in natural or man-made embayments for a few days; then, just as quickly, they disappear. Very often an ebbing tide will leave large numbers of them as gelatinous blobs along the water's edge soon to dry and vanish from sight.

In this vicinity two kinds of ctenophores are common: the one-inch-long *Pleurobrachia pileus*, the sea gooseberry, and the larger bi-lobed *Mnemiopsis leidyi*, the sea walnut. The conical, ovate, thimble-shaped *Beroe ovata* (named for a daughter of the Greek sea god, Oceanus) which lives in large swarms and is noted for its voracity, sometimes swallowing small fish and other ctenophores slightly larger than itself, is abundant from Chesapeake Bay to Florida. *Cestus veneris*, the venus girdle, is a ribbon-shaped, transparently iridescent ctenophore about 36 inches long by 3 inches wide that lives in tropical seas. Fragments sometimes are washed ashore by Gulf Stream eddies. On this coast, *Pleurobrachia* is found from Long Island to Greenland, while *Mnemiopsis* is distributed from Vineyard Sound to the Carolinas.

The first recognizable account of a ctenophore in the recorded history of biology was in 1671, and for a long time these animals were grouped indiscriminately with the jellyfish under the term Acalephae or "nettles"; later on they were placed with the coelenterates. It was not until 1889, not very long ago, that they were removed from the jellyfish, coral, hydroid phylum, and established as a separate group. The reasons for this are that compared with coelenterates, ctenophores are monomorphic (only one kind of adult); with one small exception, they lack nematocysts (stinging cells); they have significantly more highly developed muscular, digestive and sensory systems; and they have eight rows of ciliary plates, "combs," throughout life. A unique anatomical structure is the aboral (end opposite the mouth) sensory organ. This

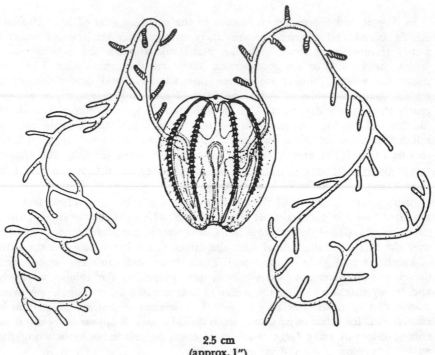

2.5 cm
(approx. 1″)

Pleurobrachia pileus—The Comb Jelly.

relatively morphologically complicated organ enables the animal to detect changes in orientation. Ctenophores are composed of 93 to 95 percent water (making them difficult to preserve); the solid material is chiefly salt with less than one percent organic material, most of which is protein.

Pleurobrachia has a pair of very long highly contractile filaments each with a series of similar short lateral branches. The filaments may be contracted at will into pitlike tentacle branches. The filaments or tentacles, are covered with adhesive cells (colloblasts) that serve to hold prey fast while the tentacles retract and draw the adhering food within reach of the mouth.

Rowing a skiff, sailing a boat or running a power boat through a swarm of ctenophores at night can produce some of the most spectacular examples of bioluminescence in the sea. In all these cases, both bow waves and stern turbulence will be outlined with brilliant flashes of blue-green light that comes from the meridional canals of whole or damaged animals. According to R. Buchsbaum, "The rapidly beating combs refract light and produce a constant play of changing colors. Comb jellies are noted for the beauty of their daytime iridescence, but this is certainly matched at night by those comb jellies that are luminescent. When the animals are disturbed as they move through the dark water, they flash along the eight rows of combs."

The high percentage of water in their tissues makes ctenophores prone to

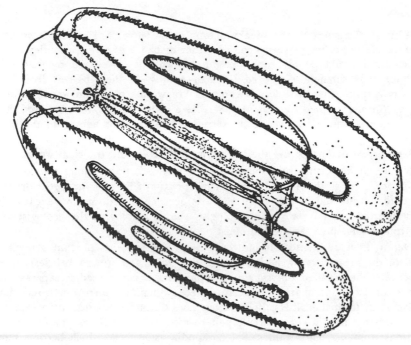

4 cm
(approx. 1⅝″)

Mnemiopsis leidyi—The Sea Walnut.

mechanically caused wounds. Such difficulties need not be fatal, since these fragile animals have a great capacity for the replacing and repairing of any part that may be damaged, destroyed or lost. Apparently all members of this group are hermaphrodites (both sexes in the same individual), ovaries and testes being found in meridional canals. Both eggs and sperm are shed into the surrounding sea through the mouth, and fertilization ordinarily takes place at once. It is quite possible and even probable that in a majority of cases self-fertilization is the rule rather than the exception. The young are also planktonic, and closely resemble the adult in form and function.

Although there are several species of ctenophores commensally associated with other organisms as gorgonians, soft corals, starfish and sea urchins, this type of existence has not been observed thus far in our coastal forms. The distribution of the commensal species may be limited by that of their hosts.

On the other hand, the long (1¼ inch), thin, pink actinarian (sea anemone), *Edwardsia leidyi*, can often be seen through the body wall of its host, *Mnemiopsis*. This is an uncommon form of biological association, a coelenterate parasitizing a ctenophore.

All ctenophores are carnivorous, living on crustaceans and other planktonic animals as well as small fishes. A large swarm of ctenophores can easily decimate all of the other zooplankton living in the same area.

Bait for Your Hooks

A stroll along nearly any breakwater or rocky outcrop of coastal New England at the right time of year, good wheather or bad, will reveal a motley crowd of young and old people concentrating on what is considered by many the activity most commonly enjoyed by man—fishing. If their bait is live, it is usually a specimen of the locally common "ragworm" or "clam worm," *Nereis virens* (formerly called *Neanthes virens*). As a matter of fact, it is believed that, apart from earthworms (which are terrestrial and do not belong to the same taxonomic group), the worms most commonly used for bait here and off the Atlantic coast of Europe are the lug worm, *Arenicola*, and the clam worm.

Nereis virens occurs from south of New England, north along the coast of Labrador, through the Arctic to the northern coasts of Europe and Great Britain. In both Europe and in this country, it has been and continues to be a favorite experimental animal for the physiologist, the embryologist, the ecologist and the comparative invertebrate anatomist.

Nereis is a segmented roundworm belonging to the phylum Annelida, and to the great class of marine worms, the Polychaeta (many bristles), more especially, the so-called *Polychaeta errantia*. This name is used to separate, for the most part, the marine free-living, free-swimming, burrowing predacious polychaetes from the others. Polychaetes have distinct segments; all except the head segment have a characteristic pair of distinctive paddle-like muscular projections from the body wall, called parapodia (side feet) which become more complicated and more highly developed toward the center of the body. Motion, breathing, and sensitivity to touch are their function. The blood-vessel-filled parapodium in *Nereis* has two easily distinguishable parts, both provided with a downward-pointing sensitive organ (cirrus), and golden-hued setae or bristles: the dorsal (upper) lobe or notopodium and the ventral (lower) lobe or neuropodium.

The head has special sense organs consisting of two dorsal tentacles, a pair of ventral palps or taste organs, four eyes, and four sense organs around the mouth. The mouth has a reversible proboscis with a few sets of lateral spines, and ends with two dark-brown, cow-horn-shaped jaws that can bite vigorously on a plane parallel with the ground. Depending on the age and size of the worm, there may be as many as 200 uniform segments behind the head, the last one bearing a pair of trailing, short, string-like sense organs. New segments are always added just in front of this terminal segment.

The clam worm is one of the largest, commonest and most colorful of our marine worms. It grows to a length of 30 centimeters or more (width about 1 cm.), and the iridescence of the upper surface of the body is greenish from which comes the species name, *virens*. They live under stones, or burrow in the sand or mud of sheltered bays where they can be collected either intertidally or just below the low tide line. When disturbed, or on the move, they swim vigorously in a serpentine motion, often playing the part of a wandering hunter, and usually thrusting the proboscis forward to seize other worms or suitable prey with their powerful jaws. A clam worm can easily destroy creatures as large or even larger than itself. Experimental work has shown that no matter

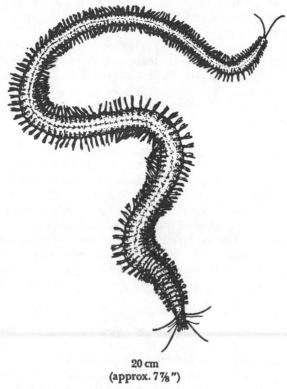

20 cm
(approx. 7⅞")

Nereis virens—The Clam Worm.

how well pieces of worms or clam meat are hidden, *Nereis* will find them. For this reason clam worms are common not only in clam flats but also in beds of the edible mussel.

In this connection, as Ricketts and Calvin have pointed out, clam worms "are very active and squirm violently when captured, protruding and withdrawing their chitinous jaws. . . . Their powerful jaws are capable of delivering a businesslike bite to tender wrists and arms (and to the tender skin between the bases of fingers), but in collecting hundreds of them barehanded we have rarely been bitten, always taking the precaution of not holding them too long."

Nereis lives in the sand in tubes whose characteristic casts can be readily recognized. The tubes are made by the extrusion of a sticky mucus from lateral glands along the body. The mucus hardens quite rapidly, at the same time incorporating adhering grains of sand from the immediate environment. This flexible tube fits the worm so closely that, using their setae (bristle-like spines) they can move within it and out of it with considerable speed. Since their habit is to leave their burrows at night, it is at this time that they become prey to fishes like the tautog and the scup which prod them out of the sand.

Since most marine worms apparently spawn in concert with tidal rhythms and with the amount of light reaching the sea, it is evident that both the sun and the moon have a profound influence on their reproductive activities. In this way, the nocturnal habit of *Nereis* swimming together in large numbers and in characteristic undulations presumably is connected with seasonal reproductive activity. The iridescent steel-blue and green males now swim in groups inshore at low tide.

It is also at this time that their appearance, together with that of the dull green, orange or reddish females, changes so radically that these sexually mature forms were thought to be a different species, and were given the name *Heteronereis*. The term "heteronereis" is now used just to denote the sexual phase. In Berrill's words, "As the season approaches, the posterior segments swell up with either egg or sperm, while the appendages normally used for creeping become changed into paddles for swimming. Then after midnight, in the dark of the moon during the summer months, the two sexes leave the sea floor and swarm to the surface of the water. Ripe males are white or gray where the sperm shows through the skin, while the back ends of the females are red with eggs. The eggs and sperm are shed into the water. When the process is over, the worms drop back to their accustomed place and in due time grow new back ends since the old and exhausted segments usually drop off." The eggs are fertilized freely in the water and the zygote (fertilized egg) develops into a typical larval stage called a trochophore. If it is not eaten by one of a large number of potential predators, the trochophore, now a member of the zooplankton, metamorphoses, becomes worm-like, and then settles to the bottom and grows into an adult *Nereis*.

Nereis virens has been discovered living in interesting association with other organisms. For example, it is now known to be a secondary host for a parasitic fluke that lives in the intestinal tract of the common eel. Experimentally, it has proven a profitable animal to use in behavior investigations. Fishermen claim that as bait, the clam worm has no rival for certain kinds of fish, and most bait dealers usually have a good supply on hand, stored on rockweed in a cool part of their stores. The mariculture of clam worms is now providing a surprisingly tidy income for many individuals of all ages living not far from tidal flats and rocky outcrops along the coast of Maine. Clam worms are so popular with anglers that they doubled in price during the past few years; they are not difficult to dig, and are easily shipped and readily stored.

A Can of Sea Worms

The world of marine worms has been known to man for as long as he has lived along the shores of salt waters. For hundreds of years, all worm-shaped invertebrates were considered to be closely related with the result that the first naturalists, and indeed many of their colleagues of later centuries, failed to notice the striking structural and environmental differences that warranted their being placed in distinct groups. So it is that the varied natural and man-made beaches and subtidal bottoms of the shoreline are inhabited by an unexpectedly large number of interesting species of unrelated groups of free-living worms. Perhaps the best known New England worms living in the sediments washed by the tides are the polychaetes (Polychaeta) whose most economically important member is the iridescent clam worm, *Nereis virens* which reaches a maximum length of about 18 inches and is a much sought bait by coastal fishermen.

Polychaetes live in sand and mudflats, and once their tracks and trails become sufficiently familiar they can be collected with relative ease. Worms, being soft bodied, self-destruct easily and should be narcotized with fresh water or Epsom salts or refrigeration, and then preserved with seven-to-ten percent neutral formalin. Worm burrows may be distinguished from other holes in the sand or mud by their characteristic piles or casts of material, their conical sunken depressions or elevated cones, or the presence or absence of bits of detritus incorporated in tubes barely extending above the sand surface.

It is not always easy to dislodge a burrowing worm. Those living in long, relatively deep tubes may be able to descend as fast as the shoveller can dig. They or their tubes may be easily broken or fragmented, or they may disappear altogether if the substrata around the dug hole caves in. The plumed worm, *Diopatra,* for instance, lives in long parchment tubes into which are woven camouflaging bits of shell, seaweed and other debris. The shovel must be pressed quickly into the sand close behind the tube of this animal with as little mechanical disturbance to the substratum as possible, and the now-unearthed tube containing the animal grasped immediately underneath to prevent the worm from rapid escape.

Polychaetes are close marine relatives of terrestrial earthworms and fresh-and-saltwater leeches, and together with these other two groups form the segmented round worms that belong to the phylum Annelida. Rings around their bodies, both internally and externally, separate annelids from all other worm groups. Polychaetes typically have paired bristle-like appendages on each segment (Polychaeta means many-bristled), and along the sides of the body there are fleshy paddle-like lobes, filaments or other paired structures which may be used for swimming, burrowing and/or respiration, depending on the species. The bristles have a great variety of shapes and are often used to distinguish one species from another. Polychaetes live in many ways: most often as tube dwellers that trap and filter their food, and sometimes as nomadic predatory animals feeding on other soft-bodied creatures. Nearly all of them have varying combinations of tentacles, antennae, cirri (slender small projections) and palps concentrated near the anterior end that provide acute senses of taste and touch, and most polychaets have at least one pair of these structures on the roof of the head.

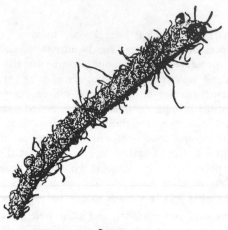

8 cm
(approx. 3⅛″)

Diopatra cuprea—The Plumed Worm. Head of the worm may be seen extending slightly from the part of the parchment tube incorporating bits of detritus that extends from sand surface.

Sexes are usually separate. Eggs and sperm are shed freely in the water, sometimes in response to temperature change, but often cyclically in tune with the tides. The eggs hatch into larvae which drift with the currents for a varying number of days before settling to the bottom and metamorphosing into adult worms.

The crawling polychaetes living beneath stones and shells on the large algae and in communities of sessile organisms such as mussels and barnacles, include such forms as *Nereis virens*, the clam worm and its close relative, *Nereis limbata*; *Cirratulus* with its long threadlike filaments that function spectacularly as gills; and the scaleworms, *Harmathöe* and *Lepidonotus*, with their peculiar dorsal, paired, platelike scales. The burrowers like *Glycera*, the beakthrower; *Lumbrinereis*; *Ophelia*; the capitellids; *Arenicola*, the lug worm; and the magnificently colored *Cirratulus*, the fringed worm, all move through the sand or sand mud substratum by peristaltic contractions.

Polychaetes live in a variety of ways; many of them have become tube dwellers. Among these are the carnivorous worms, for example, *Diopatra*, the plumed worm that incorporates fragments of its environment into its membranous three-foot tube; *Clymenella*, the bamboo worm, that lives head downward intertidally in delicate sand tubes; the beautiful fan worms or feather dusters including such common forms as *Sabella*, *Potamilla*, *Hydroides*, *Serpula* and *Spirorbis*, that build either straight tubes of sand grains and mucus or uniquely-shaped calcareous tubes attached to different kinds of surfaces. *Pectinaria*, the mason or gold-tooth worm, that builds delicate-appearing but sturdily formed tubes in the shape of ice cream cones, is conmmonly found in many of our sand flats, as is one of the most beautiful of our coastal worms, *Amphitrite ornata*, and the phosphorescent creamy-white parchment tube worm, *Chaetopterus*, that lives

5 cm
(approx. 2")

Pectinaria gouldi—The Gold Tooth Worm. The worm can be seen inside its ice cream cone shaped tube of sand with its setae ("gold teeth") protecting the entrance.

in a two-foot-long, U-shaped tube of self-manufactured parchment, often with a species of the symbiotic pea crab, *Pinnotheres,* keeping it company.

Another group of common but far less well-known marine polychaetes should at least be mentioned. These are the possibly primitive archiannelids, characteristically tiny worms that live mostly intertidally on or between the sand grains, in mud or among algae. They differ structurally from the polychaetes mostly in the possession of very few setae (bristles), the reduction or absence of parapodia and certain other appendages, and the addition of external hair-like cilia that enable them to glide on and through their tortuous habitat.

Animal behaviorists have found certain polychaetes particularly useful in studies concerning associations between animal species belonging to widely separated groups. For example, Demorest Davenport discovered a puzzling series of alliances involving food-sharing between certain scaleworms including *Harmothöe* and a variety of echinoderms including starfish, brittle stars, sea-urchins and sea cucumbers. In one case, a species of starfish was found able to release sufficient chemical attractant into the surrounding water to stimulate the approach of the polychaete from quite a distance away. It was also found that wounded or dying echinoderms had a repellant action on the scale worms, thus sparing the polychaete a relationship that would yield no food. Additional studies in this field indicated that one species of polychaete was a willing partner (commensal) with 13 kinds of animals belonging to four phyla, and that different species of small scale worms live with certain forms of tube worms, presumably sharing the food of their large, fat, soft cohabitors. A classic case of commensalism occurring between *Nereis* and certain species of hermit crabs has been investigated by inducing both the worm and the crab to accept an artificial shell of glass. According to R. V. Gotto, it was then observed that the polychaete *Nereis,* which normally occupied the upper whorls of the shell would glide forward when the crab was feeding, seize a bit of food from the crab's mandibles and quickly retreat with it to the depths of the shell.

Little Known Vermiform Denizens
of the Tidelands

Careful explorers of the mixed sand and sand sediments that cover the bottoms of a great deal of the New England shoreline will sooner or later, with careful digging, come upon members of three quite numerous but little-known groups of unsegmented worms: the ribbon worms, the peanut worms and the acorn worms. Although it is fairly easy to separate the smaller and more colorful acorn worms from the two other groups, and although grossly, ribbon worms are slightly flattened while peanut worms are quite rounded, the three kinds of worms belong to three totally different categories or phyla of the animal kingdom and are nearly entirely unrelated.

The nemertines (Nemertinea) are commonly known as ribbon worms or proboscis worms. They are a phylum of contractile soft-bodied, subcylindrical, greatly elongated worms from two inches to six feet in length. They are unsegmented and thicker and longer than flatworms. Their most unique structure is a thorn-armed proboscis contained in a sheath inside the body that can be shot out rapidly at great length from an opening close to its anterior end. The proboscis can wound and/or wrap around such living prey as mollusks, crustaceans and other worms, and draw this prey to its mouth. Most ribbon worms, especially broader types (Cerebratulus) burrow in the mud or sand, or live on rocky shores along and beneath the rocks. The narrower forms, such as Lineus, dwell in mussel beds; Tetrastemma lives on and around seaweeds, or like Oerstedia is commonly found on pilings. Some species form semipermanent burrows lined with mucus and a few live in distinct mucoid tubes of sand. A small yellowish-white worm-like form, Malacobdella, is symbiotic, and lives in the mantle cavity of the steamer clam, Mya arenaria. Cerebratulus lacteus, a white, active six-foot worm, swims at night in tidal and subtidal water with the typical undulating motion of ribbon worms.

Most nemertines move by gliding over the substratum in a trail of self-produced slime, propelled by surface cilia. Their tendency to break into pieces when disturbed or otherwise irritated can be frustrating to the collector (as it must be to preying crabs). Each of the pieces, however, has the capacity to grow into a complete animal.

For this reason nemertines have been a favorite subject for biologists interested in asexual reproduction. All species of marine nemertines copulate, the sexes are separate and they either produce their young alive, or shed eggs and sperm into the water. In any case, all pass through a free-swimming larval stage before settling to the bottom and undergoing a rather complicated metamorphosis into a young worm.

Peanut worms or sipunculids are a relatively small group of worms whose common and only representative in North Atlantic coastal waters is the often foot-long Phascolosoma gouldi, the peanut worm. According to W. D. Russel-Hunter, Golfingia, a close relative of Phascolosoma received its generic name after being discovered by the well-known zoologists, W. C. McIntosh and E. Ray Lankester, in the muddy shores of the "Royal and Ancient" golf course at St. Andrews, Scotland!

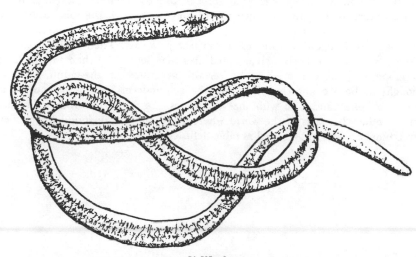

¾ life size

Cerebratulus lacteus—The largest of all American shallow-water nemerteans or ribbon worms, sometimes reaching a length of 6 meters.

Peanut worms are drab-colored, sedentary, and abundant in shallow waters. Their active burrowing in mud and sandy mud produces temporary tubes filled with mucous secretion. The unsegmented cylindrical body, through whose smooth walls longitudinal muscles may be seen, is continually expanding and contracting, making its shape quite variable. In burrowing, the animal everts its proboscis (introvert) into the sediment, enlarging this end to form a mushroom-shaped anchor, and then pulls the body toward this enlargement by contracting the strong muscles in its body wall. The introvert is an expandable, long, slender organ that can be quickly telescoped into the body when the animal is disturbed. The mouth is at the front of the introvert and is surrounded by a circlet of short ciliated tentacles in several rows. The peanut worm is both a burrower and a deposit feeder, and the water drawn toward the tentacles by the beating cilia carries minute organisms as well as sand and silt left over from construction of its tube. All of this material is trapped in mucous and swallowed. The sexes are separate; the emission of sperm by the males is said to induce females to shed their eggs, and fertilization takes place in seawater. A month later, the larvae metamorphose into young worms that settle to the bottom. Peanut worms contract quickly and must be narcotized before they are fixed and preserved by the collector.

Buried in intertidal fine sand or in muddy sand flats, and sometimes in similar substrata just below the low tide line, live the curious hermichordates or acorn worms. The only species nearby, the colorful *Saccoglossus kowalevskii*, makes its presence known by little piles of slightly coiled, easily recognized fine rope-like castings. The burrow can many times be further identified by its characteristic odor of iodoform. The wormlike body is soft, sluggish, very fragile, difficult to collect undamaged, and even more difficult to preserve whole. Acorn worms are easy to recognize by the characteristic whitish proboscis, the orange collar and the long beige trunk with easily visible paired gill slits along its entire length. The high domed, somewhat conical, proboscis within the collar resembles an acorn in its cup. As acorn worms burrow through the substratum, they swallow sand with its microscopic fauna and flora, digest the organic matter and pass the indigestible sand to the surface as a cast. Their main interest to biologists lies in the fairly well-accepted idea that because of their unique larval development and the presence of certain structures in the adult, they are thought to be a connecting link with the echinoderms (starfishes and sea urchins) on one hand, and with the vertebrates, the group to which we belong, on the other. In parts of the world where acorn worms are found in relatively large numbers they are relished as table delicacies.

New England Marine Flatworms

The minute, delicately-textured turbellarians that live among the sand grains of intertidal beaches up and down our coast are the local representatives of the group of soft-bodied free-living flatworms that belong to the phylum Platyhelminthes. Their larger relations can be found moving over sea lettuce (*Ulva lactuca*) in the tidal flats, gliding over stones and shells subtidally, swimming by rhythmic rippling motions just below the tide zone, or inhabiting empty shells of hermit crabs and whelks.

Marine flatworms are elongate, narrow, flattened, and more or less leaf-shaped. They range in length from less than half an inch to two inches, and are usually drab in color. These animals are carnivorous and the mouth, the only opening in the body, is well back from the anterior (front) end of the ventral (under) surface of the body. A tube-like proboscis (the pharynx) is extended from the mouth to the microscopic organisms—small worms, snail eggs, etc.—on which they may be feeding, and digestive juices are poured onto the food which becomes somewhat liquified before being sucked into the body. In some species, the extensible pharynx expands like a thin-walled trumpet before it envelops its prey. Flatworms glide over the bottom of submerged plants and other materials, or propel themselves through the water by nearly invisible waves of muscular contractions along with coordinated movements of their microscopic hair-like structures (cilia). They are hermaphrodites possessing both testes and ovaries, but cross-fertilization of two individuals always takes place. The eggs are laid in small patches of slender-stalked, dark-brown-to-black coccoons, usually fastened on the underside of rocks, and the free-swimming larvae become temporary members of the zooplankton. The smallest forms such as the light brown *Heptoplana* are found ordinarily under rocks near the low tideline, while the larger and more strikingly colored yellow-banded brown *Stylochus*, live mostly in dead shells. In general, flatworms may be found on and under rocks and seaweed or gliding over a variety of surfaces in their never-ending quest for food. The inch-long, spearhead-shaped, white-to-brownish-yellow species, *Bdelloura candida*, lives on the gill plates of the horseshoe crab. Behaviorists and biologists use the larger flatworms as experimental animals to study both their remarkable power of regeneration and the relationships between sense organs and movement.

In this connection, the free-living flatworms have aroused a great deal of attention. Ethologists have found from a variety of experiments with these animals that not only may they be able to store information but that past experiences may condition their future behavior. For example, after it was discovered that flatworms normally seek dark areas, and given the opportunity, will move from light to shade, they were trained by repeated physical restraints to the point where they made fewer and fewer attempts to avoid the light. More spectacular experiments showed that this kind of training could be transferred from a trained to an untrained individual by the simple expedient of feeding the trained worm to the untrained one. Perhaps the climax of this work was reached by investigators at the University of Michigan who trained flatworms, then cut them in half to find out how much acquired learning each regenerated individual retained. It turned out that the flatworm's tail has as good a memory as the head! A by-product of this and subsequent work was the researchers' publication of a now well-known journal called *The Worm Runner's Digest*. This is a mixture of fact and fun, for as the eidtor, James V. McConnell of the University of Michigan, says, "it seems to me that anyone who takes himself or his work too seriously is in a perilous state of mental health."

A few of the so-called free-living flatworms are symbiotic; that is, they spend a part or even all their life cycle more or less intimately associated with a different or larger species of animal during which there is a functional exchange. In these worms the exchange is moderate; ordinarily one partner does not depend absolutely on the other. Some of the marine forms are internal parasites in the body cavity of a species of local isopod, *Idotea*, as well as in several kinds of hermit crabs. Other parasitic turbellarians have been found in certain brittle stars (ophiuroid echinoderms); in pelecypods (bivalves) such as *teredo*, the shipworm, the mussel, *Modiolus*, and the cockle, *Cardium edule;* and in several species of gastropods (snails). It is quite possible to find a ray in the catches of local seiners and trawlers that bears on its surface the turbellarian, *Micropharynx*. However, the best known of all symbiotic flatworms are probably the predacious so-called oyster "leeches" which penetrate through the shells of the local oysters *(Crassostrea)*, and feed on the soft parts.

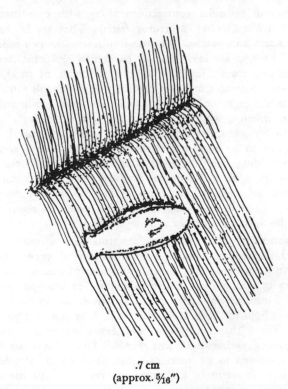

.7 cm
(approx. ⁵⁄₁₆″)

Bdelloura candida—A light brown flatworm most commonly found inhabiting the gillplates of the hermit crab.

Barnacles—The Clinging Crustaceans

The barnacle, a ubiquitous and cosmopolitan crustacean, is one of the most obvious and numerous kinds of animals found along our shores. It encrusts intertidal and subtidal rocky headlands, pilings, breakwaters, rocks and boulders, living and dead shells, and even animals such as horseshoe crabs.

Barnacles are sometimes thought of as mollusks because their bodies are entirely enclosed within a series of calcareous plates, yet their morphology during embryonic and larval development together with possession of paired jointed appendages reveals them as true arthropods belonging to the class Crustacea.

The cirrus-like or feathery feet of its better-known representatives give these marine animals the name Cirripedia. There are several readily distinguishable groups of true barnacles (order Thoracica): the Lepadomorpha or stalked forms, to which belong the goose-necked barnacles; the widely known Balanomorpha or common rock barnacles often called acorn barnacles because of their presumed resemblance to the acorn; the more distributionally restricted Verrucomorpha, smaller and asymmetrical compared with the acorn barnacles; and the three orders of curiously adapted, chitinous-clothed barnacles most of which are parastic on or within several different kinds of invertebrate hosts.

Scientific investigation of barnacles has a distinguished and interesting history starting with the Greeks, some of whom believed that geese were spawned spontaneously from certain stalked barnacles (goose-necked barnacles). Probably the best known investigator was Charles Darwin. Immediately after he returned to England from the famous voyage of the *Beagle* that was to furnish him so much material for his publications on evolution, he spent seven years producing monographs on recent and fossil barnacles. *A Monograph on the Sub-Class Cirripedia (1851-1854)* is a classic and is still the basic reference of cirripede specialists.

Louis Agassiz described the common acorn barnacles as "nothing more than a little shrimp-like animal standing on its head in a limestone house and kicking food into its mouth." In becoming permanently attached to a solid surface by its head it has lost both the eyes and sensory antennae found in more typical crustaceans. The six pairs of appendages (comparable to the locomotory limbs of other crustaceans) act as a unit; the protective valves, uppermost on the calcium carbonate skeleton separate, the feathery legs are thrust out, swept through the water and drawn back inside the valve, immediately carrying the entrapped plankton and detrital particles inside the body. This action is repeated every few seconds.

The characteristic method of reproduction in all barnacles is hermaphroditism and although each individual has both sexes, cross-fertilization is the rule. Fertilization takes place when the slender contractile sperm tube of one barnacle is thrust through the shell valves into a neighboring barnacle. Within the parent, the fertilized eggs develop into typical motile crustacean larvae and after hatching become free-living members of the zooplankton for a few weeks. Here they metamorphose into the larval stage that eventually attaches to a suitable hard surface after using principally their sensory antennae to explore and test the area. The larva employs a sticky cement secreted by an antennal gland to at-

1 cm
(approx. ⁷⁄₁₆″)

Balanus balanoides—The Common Rock Barnacle. The largest individuals on the rock are a year older than the smallest animals.

tach itself and soon thereafter a calcium carbonate skeleton is started at the base and sides.

As the animal grows, the six or eight exoskeletal calcium carbonate plates are slowly enlarged by the accumulation of additional material, while at the same time the covering of the protected internal soft parts of the body is molted or shed into the surrounding seawater. The molted skins are extremely light and are usually washed about in the water a long time before settling. Swimmers seeing these suspended in the surrounding water for the first time are nearly always sure that they have discovered a new or an extremely rare animal.

Most of the intertidal barnacles are rarely larger than a third of an inch in diameter, and may be an inch high if they are crowded together in large numbers. Smaller still are some of the parasitic forms. The largest barnacles live at some depth off the western coast of the United States with dimensions of up to nine inches high, four inches in diameter and weight of over a half a pound. Barnacles often add color to their environment ranging from white, yellow, pink, orange and red to purple with occasional striped forms.

Some kinds of barnacles always live in the littoral zone below the low-tide line; others are found at greater depths; still others live only intertidally and are able to stand temporary exposure at low tide, and finally there are forms adapted for living in the spray zone at high tide on wave-lashed rocky shores. Acorn barnacles withstand exposure when the tide is out by means of the wall of limey plates enclosing the base and body circumference and by the pair of valves on top which can be virtually sealed when necessary.

The numbers of individuals in a given area can be enormous. One has only to examine the rocky shores along any headland to note that there are thousands of these animals per square meter. This kind of super-crowding tends to induce smothering, and together with the competition sometimes offered by other sessile organisms causes considerable barnacle mortality. The barnacles higher up on the shore grow slowly and live about five years while the faster growers farther down may die after three years. In any given intertidal area the smallest barnacles are invariably the youngest.

Acorn barnacles have a variety of enemies, particularly various kinds of snails such as the dog whelk. Starfishes are also found on barnacles when other more attractive food is unobtainable. In their planktonic larval stages they are subject to predation by the larger zooplankton and by different kinds of fish.

Barnacles as fouling organisms make a costly nuisance of themselves on ship bottoms, lobster pots and various marine hardware. Before the advent of anti-fouling paints (whose efficiency against settling barnacles is partial at best), ships had been found to carry as much as 300 tons of these fouling organisms. Barnacle accumulations on hulls reduce the ship's speed considerably, increase fuel consmuption and cause frequent and costly docking. It has been estimated that the annual cost of barnacle fouling to the shipping industry in this country amounts to more than $100 million annually.

However, the barnacle-man relationship is not all on the red side of the ledger. For example, in Chile no less a person than Charles Darwin indicated that the soft parts of the barnacle are considered a delicacy and are an esteemed ingredient in soups and chowders. Waldo Schmitt, the dean of American crustacea specialists, says the "The flavor—all of its own—of this barnacle soup, as I can attest, is equal to that of the best clam chowder, while the flesh is more palatable than clam meat." One kind of goose-necked barnacle is sometimes used for food on the coasts of Brittany, Spain and Italy, while the giant West Coast barnacles are eaten by the Indians.

Callinectes sapidus, A
Favorite Target of Homo sapiens

One of the handsomest, liveliest, and most delectable animals to grace the bottoms of the shores, estuaries and bays of New England is the colorful blue crab *Callinectes sapidus*. It is an arthropod which, together with the other edible crabs, shrimps and lobsters belongs to the Decapoda or ten-footed crustaceans, the most highly developed order of the class Crusteacea.

Superficially, a blue crab seems to bear little resemblance to a lobster or shrimp, but when the folded and flattened abdomen is extended, common characters that demonstrate a relatively close relationship are revealed. Among these are the hard-shell covering of each of the 19 segments, which make the jointed protective exoskeleton, and the thin, soft intersegmental areas between, which allow mobility.

The crab's appendages display considerable structural variety; for example, the tooth-like mandibles are used to cut up tidbits presented by the outer limb-like mouth appendages, while the ten pairs of appendages following them, according to Stebbing, have the functions of "tasting and pasting, biting and fighting, grasping and clasping, walking and a kind of inarticulate talking, swimming, burrowing, besides the automatic services which they render to the eggs in the brood pouch and to the animal's own respiration." With so many units to work with, the crab has available almost any tool it needs. The fifth pair of legs in which all of the segments are broad and flattened like paddles is used as oars. This pair of swimming legs enables the blue crab to propel itself rapidly through the water, easily outdistancing its close relatives which have to get about as best they can by running along the bottom.

The blue crab and its relatives can throw off their limbs and grow new ones in their places (autotomy), a provision that doubtless provides a good method of escape from enemies. Spasmodic contraction of muscles in the second joint enables partition to take place. The nearly colorless blood coagulates quickly and the wound closes rapidly. A new limb begins to grow at once from a bud beneath the scar, and after a few molts it resembles closely the original leg.

Because of its armorlike casing, which is incapable of expansion, the crab's growth can only occur by shedding this inelastic housing. The process is called molting, and a black, white or red line down the back of the crab indicates that the animal will molt within the next few days. In this condition the crab is known to the fisherman as a "peeler." During molting, the posterior part of the body protrudes through a gap made by cracks in each side of the shell. It takes about 15 minutes for the crab to free itself completely by rhythmic throbbing movements. At this point it becomes the table delicacy known as a soft-shelled crab. Forty-eight hours later the new shell has become quite hard. Ordinarily the crab eats its discarded shell and thus gains the calcium carbonate needed to harden its new housing. Molting occurs every few weeks while the crab is young; later, shedding may take place no more than once a year. At the time of molting or shedding, the blue crab is virtually defenseless and cannot eat, which is the price these animals pay for their protective armor.

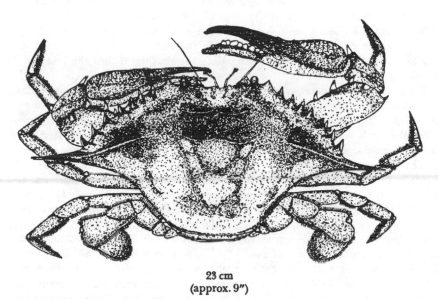

23 cm
(approx. 9″)

Callinectes sapidus—The Blue Crab.

The sexes in blue crabs and in all other decapods are separate, the larger male crab, commonly about 17 cm. wide, having a sharply pointed abdomen, while the female's abdomen is well rounded. After copulation, the female stores sperm until the eggs are ready to be deposited. She carries the eggs cemented in bunches to hairs on her swimmerets; the larger the crab the more eggs she carries; 50,000 to 2,000,000 eggs are not an uncommon burden. In this condition a crab is said to be "in sponge." The eggs hatch directly into the seawater, and eventually settle to the bottom and metamorphose into the adult form. The larval stages are all spent floating about as members of the pelagic zooplankton, subject to the predations of carnivorous plankters and small fish. Only a very few of the tens of thousands of larvae originally released by a single female ever grow to maturity.

The blue crab, one of the largest crabs on the Atlantic and Gulf coasts of the United States, ranges as far south as Uruguay. It sometimes penetrates from the ocean into fresh water, and indeed, before our estuaries became polluted, it was

39

most abundant in the brackish waters of our area. This may account for the present low blue crab population since most mating occurs in waters of low salinity. In any case, the females return to waters of relatively high salinity before the larvae hatch. Blue crabs feed on a great variety of living plants and animals (they are quite destructive to beds of small steamer clams and other thin-shelled bivalves). However, their main food seems to be dead animals, and blue crab traps or "pots" are customarily baited with dead fish. Crabs can strike with their large specialized first pair of walking legs (chelipeds) by suddenly thrusting them outward, and closing down hard with the pointed tips of their vise-like claws. The painful bite seldom does more than draw blood. It can be avoided if the crab is grasped between the bases of the swimming legs by thumb and forefinger.

The crab's stalked compound eyes are controlled separately and can be laid back into sockets in the shell at the front of the head when mechanical or other injury threatens. Passing a shadow across the eye is sufficient stimulus to trigger this protective reaction. The eyes probably form only a very crude image but are exceptionally good in determining both the movement and the location of an object.

Blue crabs have several enemies in addition to man. They are hunted along the shores and in shallow water by gulls and herons, while in deeper waters they fall victim of octopi and to fish with teeth sharp enough to crush them. The blue crab, like the lady crab and the cancer crab, retreats to deeper off-shore waters during the winter months.

The blue crabs were once of considerable economic importance in Rhode Island; unfortunately contamination of their environment in bays, estuaries, and marshes has reduced their once large, commercially valuable harvest to pitifully small numbers; indeed they have disappeared entirely from many local areas. However, they still manage to exist in fair-sized populations elsewhere along the Atlantic Coast. For example, the blue crab fishery off the Chesapeake Bay region alone yielded a catch of over 57 million pounds in 1968, of which nearly 2 million pounds were soft-shelled crabs. The total value of this blue crab fishery was about $6,786,000. Incidentally, the great variation in fresh blue crab prices at your favorite fish market is caused by their highly seasonal production, and poor storage qualities. They must be kept alive until cooked, and the fresh cooked meat has a short life of a few days at best.

The proper preparation of the blue crab for the table is an outstanding achievement in *haute cuisine*. Experienced trenchermen often associate it with a beautiful painting in an exhibition, with a prize-winning novel, or with a breath-taking musical composition. Is there greater reason to cleanse our inshore waters than to bring the blue crab population back to its former prominence?

The Crab That Solved the Housing Problem

The sharp-eyed beachcomber, splashing along just below the tide line of a sand flat or protected beach, is very often attracted to the scurrying activities of one of three species of shell-carrying crabs, commonly known as hermit crabs. This kind of crab is not only found in New England waters, but is also abundant along the water's edge from Maine to Florida, living on pebbly, sandy and muddy bottoms, in tide pools, behind sand bars, and in other shallow relatively unexposed areas.

The outstanding visible feature of the hermit crab is its shell. The shell is not part of the crab's body but belonged to a snail that had died before the crab found it. The shell protects the soft unprotected rear end (abdomen) of the crab. This part of the animal is curved in a spiral that conforms to the shape of the snail shell. In taking a shell, the crab first explores it thoroughly inside and out with claws and feet, probably to make sure it is not occupied, and then in surprisingly rapid fashion, it makes the change from its current shell to the new one.

In the southern part of New England, hermit crabs use the empty shells of snails and whelks. Favored shells are those of periwinkles, dog whelks, dove shells and mud snails. Apparently it is not the type of shell that is important to the crab, but more its size and availability. As the crab grows, the dead shell must be discarded for a larger one. If after moving into its new house, the shell proves unsuitable, the crab immediately will change back to its old home and take up the search for new housing once more. Sometimes when a crab finds a shell that for some reason seems eminently suitable but is occupied by another crab, it will make an attempt to dislodge the other crab and capture the shell for its own use. The ensuing fight is usually quite a lively affair. Crabs first move into a shell after they metamorphose on the bottom into their adult forms from their planktonic larval existence. These virtually microscopic hermit crabs easily find a shell to appropriate from the multitude of minute shells lining the bottom of the littoral and flats.

Because the body of the hermit crab is a spiral that fits the central spiral column of the shell, it is very difficult to remove the animal from the shell by just pulling it. In addition, the last pair of appendages on the abdomen are modified in the form of a clamp, thus adding to the crab's ability to maintain its position in the shell.

Hermit crabs are basically scavengers but are also known to be carnivorous and even cannibalistic, given the opportunity. Very often when one crab comes upon another that is too slow getting into a new shell, it will kill and eat its temporarily defenseless relative .

As in other crabs, the eggs are fertilized before they leave the body of the female. As the eggs are extruded by the female they are attached to small appendages of the tail by a sticky proteinaceous material that she produces. However, because of the spiral curve of her body they are cradled on the left side of the abdomen rather than in the center as in other kinds of crabs. The eggs of hermit crabs are often brilliantly colored in various shades of orange or dark purple. When danger seems past she will often come far enough out of her shell to wave the egg masses, thus both aerating and cleaning them at the same time. She also emerges at hatching time and nudges off the young with a setose brush-like appendage on her left side.

Male hermit crabs are usually larger and much more pugnacious than females, and ordinarily there is a great deal of spirited fighting for the favor of the more desirable females. After beating down the opposition, a male will probably drag the shell of a female until she is ready to shed. After this happens he immediately deposits his sperm inside her shell and onto her abdomen. This insures fertilization of the eggs as they emerge.

Ecologists and others interested in animal associations have observed that shells occupied by hermit crabs are often apparently unusually suitable places for the settling of a variety of other organisms. In one case there is a species of hermit crab that is always found with a sea anemone attached to its shell. The anemone has a broad base which is wrapped around the shell, its mouth, surrounded by tentacles, being on the underside next to the shell opening. Presumably the anemone affords protection to the hermit and in return shares in gathering up the bits and pieces from the hermit crab's meals. When the hermit crab moves to a new shell it detaches the anemone from the o!d shell with its chelate claws and places it on the new shell. However, in this partnership, it is not always necessary for the hermit crab to move to a larger shell as it grows, since the enveloping and similarly growing anemone may extend beyond the opening of the shell thus increasing the size of the hermit crab's home. As time passes, the anemone may dissolve the shell so that the hermit crab becomes enveloped in a soft fleshy mantle that is actually part of the anemone's body.

In another example, the smooth rounded yellow lumps of a common local species of sponge dredged from a few fathoms of water may have a round opening in which the claws of a small hermit crab may be seen. When the sponge is cut open the body of the hermit crab is found resting in a spiral cavity at whose apex is the remains of the shell, the shell having been dissolved by the sponge which had originally settled on it and then replaced it.

Some hermit crabs often have colonies of small hydroids, particularly those of the genus *Hydractinia* attached to the shells they carry, giving the shells a sort of velvety appearance when the hydroid individuals are expanded. These species of hydroids may also be found attached to rocks and to sea weeds. However, when *Hydractinia* colonies are carried by hermit crabs they always develop an additional type of spiral zooid (individual) thought to be protective in function.

Other organisms that may settle on hermit crab shells are barnacles, flattened limpet types of mollusks, algae, etc. In these cases, no special types of relationships have been observed between these occasional and often chance settlers and the hermit crabs.

As might be imagined, zoologists interested in investigating animal behavior have paid considerable attention to the biology and activities of hermit crabs, and a relatively large amount of literature is building about these active and apparently always busy little animals in the research libraries of the world. Many Italians have given such investigations a more personal and practical touch by cooking the crabs in oil. When done they are served in the shell and taken out with a pin or a toothpick to be eaten.

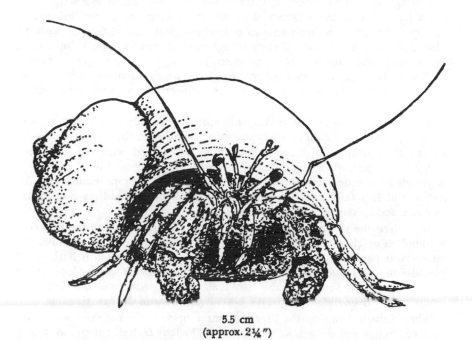

5.5 cm
(approx. 2¼")

Pagurus pollicaris—The Large or Warty Hermit Crab. This individual is living in the shell of a moon snail.

And Other Crabs

Barring the shelled mollusks, there is probably no animal more typical or more suggestive of the seashore than the crab. Even the mere dining-room zoologist who knows animals only as gastronomic delicacies is familiar with the blue crab. To the naturalist, *Callinectes sapidus* has another appeal. Out among its haunts in the salt water bays and inlets, clinging idly to a tangle of seaweed or lording it along the sandy bottom over its less well offensively endowed fellow invertebrates, the blue crab is a colorful object that attracts immediate attention.

Although the blue crab is strikingly handsome, the lady crab could, without stretching the term, be called really beautiful. The lady crab, *Ovalipes ocellatus*, has a velvet costume of delicate greenish-yellow flecked with red and ornamented with peacock eyes of closely strippled purple dots. The dorsal shield is gracefully rounded, the claws symmetrical and nicely proportioned, and the last pair of legs fashioned into oval swimming plates that add grace to its appearance and serve it well in its aquatic habitat.

As is often the case with animals with such striking coloration, the lady crab is found on or close to sandy beaches, spending much time in the shallows and on occasion parading over the exposed area of shore. More often it buries itself partially in the loose sand, its stalked darting eyes always on the lookout for prey or intruders. Sometimes the lady crab ventures out from the shore and swims rapidly over the surface of the bottom just beyond the low tide line.

When disturbed out on the beach, it cuts a furrow into the sand with sharp oar-like flippers and sinks down out of sight. The lady crab disappears so rapidly that it is difficult to believe an animal with this shape can dig out of sight apparently instantaneously. This burrowing habit is very useful for all marine animals that venture on exposed beaches. By sinking into the sand, they are protected against the crashing breakers during a storm.

The lady crab is expert at catching small fishes. A school of minnows flashes by. There is a dart of eager claws and the fishes pass on minus one of their number. The captive is disposed of head first, and the lady crab sinks back into ambush with only its alert knobby eyes protruding on their long stalks.

Wanderers along the seashore often notice *Carcinides maenas*, a mottled olive-green crab with a comb of ten teeth along the front of the dorsal shield. Called the "green crab," it is found in both brackish and saline habitats and is at home on the other side of the Atlantic as well as along the New England Coast. Because it is so active and pugnacious, the French call it "Le crabbe enragé." Confined with other species, he often runs amuck and indulges in wholesale slaughter, yet when his mate is about to shed her protective armor, he will stand guard over her. It is an interesting sight to come upon a hard-shelled male crab clinging to its soft-shelled partner and protecting her during the molting period when she is quite defenseless.

If you are so unfortunate as to be gripped by the crushing pincer of a green crab, try to forget the pain by musing over the fact that the creature probably is exerting a pull of about two kilograms, a force equivavlent to nearly thirty times the weight of its own body. The average hand grip of a man is capable

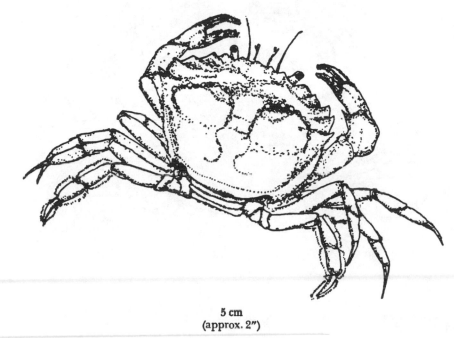

5 cm
(approx. 2″)

Carcinides maenas—The Green Crab.

of a fifty-kilogram pull, about two-thirds of his own weight. If a man had as much relative strength in his grip as a crab, hand-clasping as a sign of friendship would soon be prohibited!

Somewhat similar in appearance to the green crab are the various species of small mud crabs, olive-brown in color with large powerful claws often tipped with black. To this group belong several closely resembled species of the genus *Panopeus*. They abound in muddy localities, under stones and hiding among masses of sponges, seaweeds, discarded cans and other artifacts. Mud crabs are for the most part quiescent, lounging in a protected environment, lethargically living and letting live. When uncovered or detected under a stone, they either remain motionless or arouse themselves and scramble away.

A large and noticeable coastal crab is the rock crab. Its shell, which grows to be five inches wide, is yellowish in color, thickly stippled with reddish dots, and bordered along the forward edge with nine blunt teeth. It has a broad body and heavy claws. This crab lives in the shallow water close to the shore and when the tide is out, can often be found under stones, in rocky crevices, or buried beneath the sand or gravel. Though edible in the winter months when they molt, their flesh is not as delicate or as highly esteemed as that of the blue crab.

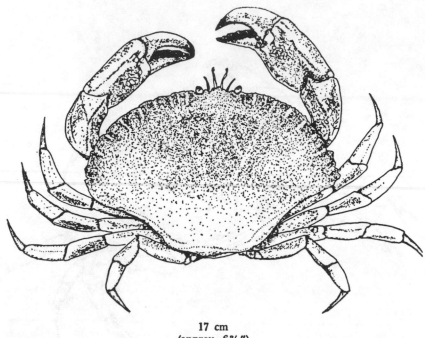

17 cm
(approx. 6¾")

Cancer borealis—The Northern or Jonah Crab.

Heavier and more massive than the rock crab, but quite similar in appearance, is its relative, the Jonah crab. A dull, brick-red color and stony texture give the crab an appearance of power and hardness. Enormously rugged but stubby claws add to the impression of strength. Relying on its size, its toughness and the strength of its black pincers, it does not often seek refuge in shelter. Boldly clinging to a ledge or point of rock, it resists the onset of the waves. In addition to man, its greatest enemies are the herring and black-backed gulls that wheel and scream along the Atlantic coast. These voracious birds carry off many a bold Jonah to satisfy their large appetites.

The Jonah crab is no swimmer and neither is the rock crab. Both crawl along on their pointed legs, progressing sidewise as is the mode of all true crabs, pulling with one set of legs and pushing with those opposite. In spite of their awkward appearance and bow legs, they cover ground at a fair pace.

Cancer is the ancient Greek name for crab. It is now the generic name of both the rock and Jonah crab. The former is *Cancer irroratus*, "the besprinkled one" and the latter is *Cancer borealis*, the "cancer crab of the North." In old mythology, Cancer was the crab commissioned by Juno to plague Hercules when he was in the Lernean swamp battling its fierce denizen, the many-headed serpent. Hercules, however, crushed the crab with a single blow. Juno, in true queenly fashion, "knighted" the crab by placing it in the evening sky, making it into a constellation visible to anyone with sufficient imagination.

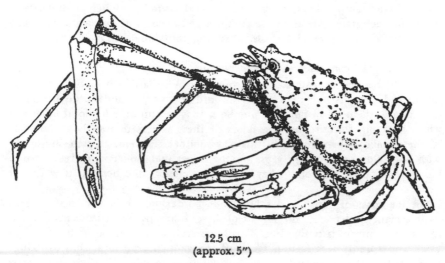

12.5 cm
(approx. 5")

Libinia emarginata—The Common Spider Crab.

In considerable contrast to these large, active, colorful crustaceans are the scrawny, slow-moving, cosmopolitan, omnivorous, spider crabs—*Libinia dubia* with six small spines down the center of its back, and *Libinia emarginata* with nine spines in the same position. They are strange caricatures, having humpy, bulging, toad-shaped bodies with skinny legs and emaciated claws. Spiders they are to the extent of having long, slender legs, but so weak and sluggish are they that here the comparison ends.

Spider crabs are prodigious gatherers of moss and therein probably rests their salvation. Their bodies, covered with chitinous hairs, become coated with a bacterial or diatomaceous ooze which encourages the growth of larger algae, as well as hydroids, tube worms and other marine invertebrates. This coating is often an excellent camouflage, offering protection from predatory neighbors.

Not only does the spider crab passively encourage the growth of a marine garden on its carapace, but it is frequently the gardener who plants the vegetation there. This crab has been observed to snip off bits of sponge, sprays of *Bugula* (a low, branching byrozoan), hydroids, or even fronds of seaweeds and actually place them into position on its back, head or legs. The cut ends are first touched to the mouth, smeared with oral cement, and then glued into place or caught in the fine hairs which mat its dorsal surface. When the spider crab changes its environment, it may modify its make-up in tune with the character of its new surroundings.

This masking habit or camouflage has been studied by zoologists interested in animal behavior. It is a device undoubtedly used in defense, but it is apparently equally important as an offense strategy, enabling the crab to steal upon its prey unnoticed or to lie in wait for it unseen. The dramatic episode of Birnam Wood marching on Dunsinane is a relatively common occurrence on the bottoms of our marine embayments where spider crabs and other invertebrates often stalk their prey.

Spider crabs are very numerous in our shallow marine ponds and may be found often in large numbers along the bottom of upper Narragansett Bay. They wander slowly about the bottom on their stilt legs, loiter in underwater prairies of eel grass or poke in the crannies and crevices of disintegrating litters of pelecypod and gastropod shells. Shedding individuals cling to the tops of clumps of *Zostera marina* (eel grass) close to the surface, a surfacing phenomenon that may be connected with their molting.

Out in the deeper waters of our sounds as Vineyard, Rhode Island, Block Island and Long Island, the spider crabs are also very abundant. Oyster fishermen dredge them up in immense numbers. It is not unusual for local fishermen while mopping starfish from the floors of these waters to trap large numbers of these crabs. When caught in this way, neither the females, some burdened with huge clusters of orange eggs, nor the larger males offer much resistance to handling. Thown overboard, they sink like stones to the bottom; they cannot swim.

Off the coast of Japan and other lands bordering the North Pacific Ocean lives a giant spider crab, the largest of all crustaceans. With legs outspread, it can span as much as twelve feet. This huge crab seems almost mythical, yet its weak and spindly legs furnish much of the canned crab meat sold as "king" crab. Its body never exceeds a foot in length or breadth. Though frightening in appearance, it is apparently no special menace to the fisherman in whose lines it occasionally becomes entangled.

Most New Englanders who are fond of eating oysters and mussels have come across the very small pink crustaceans which sometimes add a touch of color to the oyster stew. These are *Pinnotheres maculatus,* the pea crabs: curious, sluggish, pillow-shaped crabs no larger than a garden pea. In the Northeast, they usually live commensally (in partnership) with oysters (oyster crabs) or mussels (mussel crabs), and in the worm tubes of both the parchment tube worm, *Chaetopterus,* and the ornate worm, *Amphitrite.*

In other parts of the coastal United States certain species of pea crabs live in the tubes of a variety of worms; some cohabit in the burrows of the mud shrimp; some inhabit the gill baskets of large sea squirts; some live on the under surface of cake urchins; still others dwell in paper clams and keyhole limpets. In many cases each species has its own species of host.

Pea crabs are not harmful, and in several parts of the world they are considered great delicacies. They have relatively small legs, rudimentary eyes, and are one-half to one inch across. The female pea crab lives safely housed between the gills in the mussel or oyster mantle cavity—one crab to one shellfish. The mantle cavity is really part of the outer surface of the animal, although it appears to be internal. This space contains the gills and foot of the shellfish. She cannot leave because when she is mature she is too large to escape from her adpoted home.

The male is a minute, typically wandering, more round-shaped, free-swimmer in a hard black shell. Their mating was a mystery for many years, until it was observed that the smaller male enters the living bivalve host of the female, mates with her, and then moves on to repeat his performance elsewhere. She then produces fertilized eggs and carries them in the usual way until they hatch and are released to the surrounding seawater, where the pea crab larvae become temporary members of the zooplankton.

Interestingly, when metamorphosis takes place, the body structure of the first crab stage is modified and becomes structurally adapted for reaching the host with the incoming current of water that brings the bivalve its food and oxygen.

According to the observations of G. E. and N. MacGinnitie, who put glass windows in the shell of a mussel and were able to watch the activities of one of these pea crabs, they "obtain their food by eating some of the mucous string by means of which the mussel carries food to its mouth." More commonly they are thought to take their food from the incoming food supply of the host mollusk.

Some zoologists believe that a pea crab is a true parasite, because while it is in the host, its body appears to degenerate becoming far softer than when it first invaded the bivalve, and its locomotive powers seem to decrease. There is also evidence that while *Pinnotheres* is in the mantle cavity of its host, there may be erosions of the host's gills, palps and other structures.

In the u-shaped parchment tube of the large marine worm, *Chaetopterus,* there lives a very small crab, *Pinnixa chaetopterana,* commensally with the worm. The worm builds a recurved tube nearly two feet long in the sand with both ends open and projecting just above the surface, a few inches apart. The bend of the tube is roomy and swollen, but the openings are so small that neither worm nor crab can ever make their escape. Using its own secretion, the worm surrounded itself with the tube and thus became a prisoner, while the crab entered the tube when it was a larva and after metamorphosing into an adult became too large to escape.

Man is naturally a gregarious animal, and perhaps for this reason great congregations always arouse his interest. So it is that the fiddler crabs by sheer force of numbers have attracted considerable attention.

Above the high water line and in the area between tide marks, in salt marshes, on mud and sand flats or where tall spartina grass grows in stiff, green spears, fiddler crabs riddle the sand with innumerable burrows. In such areas along the margin of the beach when the tide is out, a horde of little crabs will scuttle away when disturbed, retreating shoreward to hide in muddy crevices or to seek the safety of their one-to-two-foot-deep tunnels. Very often the droves of these crabs is so large that their rapid scurrying among the grassy clumps and thickets rustles audibly.

A cursory examination reveals that these crabs may be divided into two groups, some with two small front claws and the others bearing one small and one extremely large claw. The former are females, the latter males. The males have the habit of slowly waving the large claw back and forth. The fancied resemblence of this activity to that of a bowing bass viol player is responsible for the name "fiddler." The great claw, usually on the right side, is strictly a weapon of defense. The crab eats with the small claw, picking up with it bits of algae; its burrow is dug with the walking legs. When coming out of its tun-

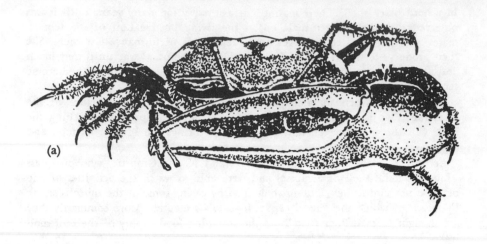

(a)

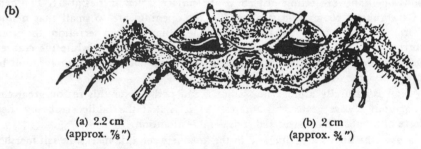

(b)

| (a) 2.2 cm | (b) 2 cm |
| (approx. ⅞″) | (approx. ¾″) |

Uca pugnax—The Fiddler Crab. (a) Male. (b) Female.

nel, the giant claw appears first and when it is retreating into the burrow the claw enters last.

The mud flats where fiddlers live are punctured with innumerable small holes, entrances to their burrows. In excavating these, the crabs scrape together large pellets of mud and sand which they bring out of the tunnels and scatter far away from the entrances. The smaller pellets strewn about in profusion in the same area are fecal droppings. Although fiddlers do not actually eat the sand, they are presumed to sift the grains with their mouth parts, picking out the nutrient materials mixed up with it.

Uca is the generic name of the Fiddler Crab. In our waters there are three species: *pugnax*, "the fighter" (common in salt marshes) ; *minax;* and *pugilator,* "the threatener," largest of the three, and usually farthest away from the salt water, being frequently where the water is brackish.

50

Hippa talpoida, the mole crab or sand bug, is a small, light-brown-to-white-tinged-with-purple, cylindrical beast that lives sometimes in large numbers between the tide lines on open beaches. The male *Hippa,* lives buried from sight and so is rarely seen by summer visitors to the seashore. To see these crabs one must dig into the exposed sand near low water mark along the beaches.

Hippa is only about an inch long. Its body is smooth and barrel-shaped, its legs short but fashioned into capable instruments for burrowing, which it accomplishes with great rapidity by pushing backwards and downwards into the sand. It is aided in this activity by a specialized elongated triangular shovel-shaped telson. Without the powerful claws of other crabs and suffering from soft and much reduced mouth parts, it lives by swallowing large quantities of sand, leaving to its internal organs the task of extracting the large numbers of minute animals and algae that live in the interstices between the sand grains.

The mole crab has a remarkable pair of plumed and pliant antennae. They number over a hundred segments, each joint bearing a fringe of from eight to twelve long hairs. The crab generally holds these delicate plumes concealed under its body. It is thought that in addition to being sensory, they are used to clean particles from other organs and appendages. Doubtless, they perform some sensory function as well. Its plumose feet prevent it from sinking too rapidly when the beach is flooded.

Together with the blue crab and the hermit crab, these are probably the marine crabs found in greatest numbers along our shores.

Freshwater Shellfish Delicacy

The common crayfish, crawfish, crawdads, or crabs as they are variously known are the only true freshwater decapods found in New England rivers, large and small, as well as in many lakes and ponds. They live best in streams that course over limestone somewhere along their upper reaches and in the ponds into which they empty.

The structure and behavior of the crayfish is remarkably similar to that of the lobster, but it differs in its development by having no free-swimming larval stage and is only four to five inches long. The adults can live out of water for weeks if they are kept moist and cool; however, the natural means of dispersal of crayfish are very limited, the eggs being carried by the female. The young when hatched have all the appendages of the adult except two pairs of abdominal appendages.

Certain species have become adapted to almost terrestrial habits. A number of them in the United States are often found at considerable distances from open water, burrowing in the damp meadows, their burrows reaching down to the water table. Other kinds erect chimney-like piles of mud at the mouths of their burrows, and in places like these their characteristic chimneys are so numerous that in times not too long past, they were said to "hamper farming operations by interfering with the harvesting machines, clogging and ruining them!"

Male and female adult crayfish are easily distinguished: males usually have larger claws and narrower abdomens, and the minute cup-like genital opening is found on the base of the fifth pair of legs rather than at the base of the third pair of legs as in females. At one of the lower joints of all of the walking legs is a "breaking point" where a crayfish when grabbed can break off its leg. Missing legs are nearly always regenerated.

Body color varies from dark brown through red, orange, green and more rarely, blue, with shades in between. Usually newly molted specimens are more brightly colored than older specimens. In general it can be said that their color varies with the background of their substratum.

Crayfish are omnivorous, eating succulent aquatic plants in preference to animal food (preferred live or freshly killed). Adults usually remain hidden under stones and other bottom debris in shallow waters from three to five feet during the day, but between dusk and dawn they come out and feed. When it is cloudy and when streams are shaded they may emerge from their hiding places and wander about during the day.

Crayfish live in many different ponds and streams, and it is suspected that there are as many more species of native crayfish as there are kinds released from the bait buckets of bass fishermen. Surprisingly, no survey of the crayfish of Rhode Island has been made, although much is known about these decaponds in some neighboring states. In any case, all of them are equally delicious when prepared for the table.

Crayfish may be collected with long-handled dip nets, minnow seines, minnow traps, and by examining overhanging banks, masses of vegetation and the undersides of submerged logs and stones. Best results are often obtained by hunting them at night with a headlamp.

Lobster Lore,
The American Lobster

*'Tis the voice of the Lobster: I heard him declare,
"you have baked me too brown, I must sugar my hair."*
Lewis Carroll, in *Alice in Wonderland*

The popularity of the American lobster, *Homarus americanus*, as a table delicacy the length and breadth of boreal North America, is probably responsible for the unusual interest in this crustacean's life and times. This is reflected not only in the great amount of research on its biology, distribution and value in the marketplace, but also in its culture and commercial development by individuals and shellfish firms. The best known and most informative early work on the biology of the lobster was a monograph by F. H. Herrick in the first decade of this century, "The Natural History of the American Lobster." Since then, a veritable "five-foot shelf" of publications has appeared on this most important food crustacean. The annual lobster catch not too many years ago amounted to over 100,000,000 individuals, but is now much less for many reasons, including overexploitation, and increased efficiency in collecting methods without sufficient catch-limitation and enforcement. At today's prices, lobsters are luxury items.

Those who travel to the southern United States and to the Caribbean Islands may be confused by the apearance of "spiny lobster" on the menus. *Panulirus argus* is a very different animal from *Homarus*. It is smaller, has a great many spines all over its body, lacks the powerful claws of its northern relative, and only its muscle-filled abdomen is eaten.

Homarus lives in rock ledges and crevices and along rocky bottoms the length of the New England coast, in the entrances to the larger bays, in many of the sounds, and in other waters with suitable depth and sufficient food. Ordinarily it is a dark greenish or reddish purple, although very occasionally a striking light blue or green lobster is caught in a trap or speared by a scuba diver. In any case, they all turn bright red when boiled or when they are preserved. Lobsters are scavengers and will feed on all manner of organic matter from seaweed to dead fish, a fact that is taken advantage of when lobster fishermen bait their pots. Live food including the softer-shelled bivalves (clams and mussels), are also acceptable, as are bones of fish and parts of clam shells, but it is a rare occasion when the lobster's relatively slow movements result in the capture of a very active animal like a small bottom fish. Their main enemies appear to be man and codfish. The lobsters in this area seem to be divided into two size-groups. The smaller ones live near the shore at shallow depths and the larger—up to more than 45 pounds—are collected by draggers in deeper waters offshore. With the ever-increasing pressures of commercial lobstering, the average overall size of both groups of lobsters has decreased. Investigations by personnel of the Narragansett Marine Laboratory at the University of Rhode Island indicated that the small coastal lobsters may be a separate race from the giants that live at 200 fathoms.

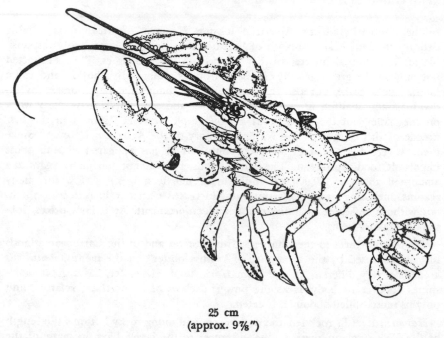

25 cm
(approx. 9⅞")

Homarus americanus—The American Lobster. The average length of the adult lobster collected for the market is 25 centimeters (.45 to .65 kilograms) although offshore specimens weighing more than 20 kilograms have been captured.

The lobster is an excellent example of an animal with an exoskeleton (shell), compared with an animal like man with an endoskeleton (bones). The exoskeleton protects the internal organs and the other soft tissues, and in addition, its lining serves as the rigid attachment area for the body muscles. Further, the hard shell makes possible a jointed armor exemplified by legs, claws and other appendages. Since the shell is inelastic and will not accommodate growth, it has to be molted or shed if the animal is to increase in size. In molting, an ever-widening split occurs along the top of the abdomen (tail), and the lobster lies on its side, bends its body in the shape of a V, backs out slowly, drawing along all of its soft parts, and crawls away to hide until its new shell is hardened. During this period, its soft mouth parts prevent it from eating. Just before the shell hardens, the growth substances absorb water quickly and the body expands depending on how well it has fed. When the shell is molted, toxic wastes produced by the body are discarded at the same time.

The common mode of progression is walking, using the four pairs of legs.

This is accomplished quite deliberately and carefully with the aid of the sensitive divining of the forward-waving antennae. However, lobsters can also swim, after a fashion, when sufficiently provoked or when they are away from protective outcrops of the substrate. In swimming, they flip their tails forward violently and are shot backward precipitously.

The lobster sexes are separate, and in mating, the hard-shelled male impregnates the soft-shelled female within a few hours after she has shed. The sperm remains viable in the body of the female for at least nine months, until she spawns. In spawning, the eggs flow from openings in the female's body over the receptacle on her body where the sperm are stored. At this point, the eggs are fertilized. They are then attached to the mother's swimmerets by a natural adhesive, and here they remain protected and aerated throughout an incubation period of ten to eleven months. A lobster lays from 3,000 eggs (7-inch female), to about 10,000 (10-inch female, 1¾ pounds), to about 75,000 (18-inch females). Female lobsters carrying eggs are known as "berried" lobsters. When newly hatched, the larvae are planktonic (floating) and go through several molts in the two months before they settle to the bottom. Young lobsters remain inshore during the summer, and with cold weather, migrate into deeper water.

The one-pound lobster is called a "chicken" lobster even though it may be as much as six years old. It takes about five or six chicken lobsters to make one pound of lobster meat. Lobsters weighing over two-and-a-half pounds are called "jumbos." Opinion differs concerning the proper method of boiling a lobster. Many believe that the tenderest meat is produced by placing the live lobster in a roomy container, covering it with cold tap water, adding one tablespoon salt, boiling for five minutes and simmering for several minutes more, depending on its size.

The Native Shrimp

Relatively few New Englanders are acquainted with the fact that in certain areas of their bays and salt ponds, and especially in the embayments lining the coast, there are pockets of small varieties of deliciously edible shrimp. Although these animals are neither present in marketable quantities nor are they nearly as large as the commercially available "pink," and "brown" shrimp, they are in sufficiently large numbers for canapes or for salads.

Shrimps are arthropods in the class Crustacea and subclass Malacostraca and belong to a well-defined and equally well-known order, the Decapoda or ten-footed crustaceans. This order includes crayfish, lobsters and crabs. In common with their fellow decapods, shrimp are characterized by the possession of a seg-mented external skeleton made basically of chitin, whose thin and softer jointed areas permit the parts to move backwards and forwards; 19 true appendage-bearing segments or somites; stalked eyes, and a posterior terminal telson. In shrimp, the laterally compressed body is divided into three main regions, the head, thorax and abdomen of which the first two (head and thorax) cannot be recognized separately because they are coalesced and are covered by a single dorsal shield, the carapace. While built on a uniform structural plan, the paired segmented appendages have become adapted to a variety of functions: the first two are the feelers (antennules and antennae); the third pair, just out-side the mouth, are the jaws (mandibles); the fourth and fifth pair are ac-cessory jaws (maxillae); the sixth through the eighth pairs are the so-called jaw feet that assist ingestion (maxillipeds); the next five pairs of appendages are the walking legs, one or more pairs of which may be clawed, the following five pairs of appendages on the abdomen are the swimmerets (pleopods), and the last pair of appendages are the uropods, which together with the telson, form the tail-fan. With so many units of such varied design, it is little wonder that decapods are able to become involved in a large number of activities.

One of the more startling aspects of decapod biology is the ability to cast off a leg and grow a new one in its place (autotomy). This capacity for limb regeneration is well known in crabs and lobsters, but has not been well docu-mented in shrimps. Since a new limb ordinarily becomes indistinguishable from its predecessor after a few molts, the primary importance of molting in the life history of a shrimp should be indicated. The hard shell of the shrimp is in-capable of expansion and, if the animal is to grow, it becomes necessary to shed this suit of armor periodically. The animal accomplishes this by backing out through a transverse slit along the posterior part of the carapace, shedding not only the shell but also the lining of its stomach and the terminal part of its intestinal tract. As may be easily imagined, molting is not only a dangerous and exhausting process for the decapod, but it also exposes the individual to its natural predators. Ordinarily, shrimp eat their shed exoskeleton, presumably deriving in this way the necessary lime salts for the rapid hardening of the new shell. Between molts, shrimp eat almost anything including algae, small crusta-ceans, worms, larvae and small fish, and in some instances they are apparently excellent scavengers.

The exoskeletons of the small local shrimp are semi-transparent making

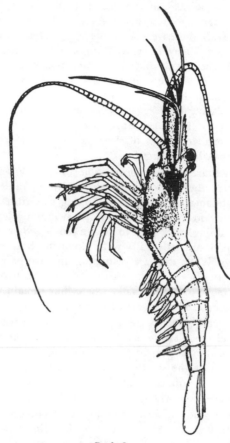

Body 3 cm
(approx. 1¼″)

A young penaeid shrimp.

visible through the carapace the more or less elliptical bulbous heart. It is easy, and fascinating, to see the rapidly beating heart of a native shrimp after it is caught and put in a small clean glass jar of seawater.

As would be expected in active animals, the sense organs of shrimp are well developed. Each of the antennules has three branches which are constantly in motion searching the immediate environment. The two long branches extend the entire body length, and sometimes farther. The antennae are about half the length of the body and are ordinarily trailed backwards along the sides. The eyes are noticeably large and carried on movable stalks. The pointed and sometimes spined forward extension of the carapace between the eyes is the rostrum, a structure of considerable diagnostic significance.

57

Shrimp, as all other decapods, have separate sexes. The external opening for the passage of sperm is near the basal segments of the last pair of legs in the males; in the female, the eggs come from gonoduct openings near the bases of the third from the last pair of legs. The female often has a special organ called a sperm receptacle in which she stores the sperm from the male until the eggs are ready to be deposited. Females in most species of shrimps carry the eggs after extrusion on their swimmerets, each egg being cemented with material associated with the covering of the egg. A female shrimp "in berry" (carrying fertilized eggs) may carry 2,000 eggs. They hatch as a special kind of planktonic larva, the zoea, which later metamorphoses to the adult. Soon after the eggs have hatched, the female molts; sometimes she may spawn twice during one season. Most berried females travel seaward before their broods hatch. Here again, placing local egg-carrying female shrimp in a clean glass jar with seawater will reveal in its amazing entirety and color the developing egg mass. Some of the smaller species of shrimps are able to change their sex as they grow, being first male and later female.

Shrimps and prawns are able swimmers as anyone knows who has tried to net them. When alarmed, they can move backward quite rapidly by folding the tail-fan under the abdomen and suddenly flipping it. Ordinarily they swim forward by means of the five pairs of abdominal swimming legs with bristles on the inner edges enabling each pair to be locked together as though holding hands. Some shrimps characteristically walk along the bottom, using only their last two pairs of legs. When they are swimming, the five pairs of swimming legs beat in graceful rhythmic succession. In the fall, as the temperature begins to drop, many species move to deeper water where they remain until the following spring when the water starts to become warm again.

There is a difference between a shrimp and a prawn although both terms refer to similar animals in a sub-group of the decapods, the Natantia. "Prawn" is a name given for the larger kinds of swimming shrimps, while the term, "shrimp," refers to all of the smaller types. In general, the body of a shrimp compared with that of a prawn is more flattened when seen from above, its right and left limbs are more widely seperated, and it lacks a prominent rostrum.

Three of the many kinds of shrimps along the Atlantic Coast, many of them with unusual habits, are usually common in New England waters. *Hippolyte (Virbius) zostericola* is a smaller translucent shrimp, mottled greenish and brown, sometimes spotted with red, sometimes entirely green, found as the species names indicates, living in or close to patches of eelgrass. In addition to the color, one of the easiest means of identification is the sharp almost perpendicular bend of the abdomen at the third segment. It ranges from Vineyard Sound in Massachusetts to the southern coast of New Jersey, and may be collected by running a fairly coarse dip-net through patches of eelgrass.

Palaemonetes vulgaris is the common prawn. The adults are much larger than *Hippolyte* and are translucent with brownish spots. It also occurs in eelgrass but more often lives in ditches, salt marshes and similar places, in many instances being found over mud-sand bottoms. It is distributed along the Atlantic Coast from New Hampshire southward.

Crangon septemspinosus, the most abundant of the three shrimps, is a translucent pale gray animal with minute star-shaped dark spots. It is found from Labrador to North Carolina, its numbers diminishing as its southern limit is approached. This is the common sand shrimp, a decapod that usually occurs in large numbers on sand flats and deeper water-sand sediments farther off shore. It has also been collected from tide pools. It is a relatively hardy combination of scavenger and carnivore that lives well in a marine aquarium. One can readily observe there that its translucent grayness is a beautiful camouflage when it is resting motionless on the sand bottom, or partially buried in the sand. The method by which this and related shrimps change color involves large numbers of chromatophores which are under hormonal control, the hormones being produced in ductless glands in the eyestalks. When caught intertidally on an ebbing tide, it may be found burrowed several centimeters into the moist sand. Examination of stomach contents reveal it to be one of the foods of bluefish, flounders, striped bass, and other fishes frequenting its habitat.

Although it does not occur in these waters, mention should be made of *Peneus setiferus,* the peneid shrimp or prawn, commonly found in the freezing compartments of grocery stores and supermarkets. The peneids are the most important market species of shrimp. In 1971 the total United States catch of these "pink" and "brown" shrimp was roughly 234 million pounds, heads-off weight, worth about $166.2 million to the fishermen who landed them. This is easily the most valuable fishery in the United States.

Recipes for preparing shrimp are as delicious as they are numerous. The shrimps from the coastal waters may be used for nearly all of them.

The Horseshoe Crab—A Living Fossil

For more than 200 million years, since the Triassic Period, horseshoe crabs identical with those touring the shores of our bays have struggled from the sea. They belong to one of the oldest known living varieties of creatures—so old that their only close relatives are fossils extinct for millions of years. For these reasons they are known to zoologists as "living fossils."

Anyone who has spent much time swimming in harbors or collecting quahogs, steamers or mussels knows the horseshoe crab, *Limulus polyphemus*. One of nature's most successful animals, it is a broad, flat dark creature with a long spike tail. Turned over, its shell rim looks like a perfect horseshoe. Although women often scream when they step on one of them while wading, the horseshoe crab is harmless.

Continents have shifted. Ocean bottoms have become mountain ridges. Nearly everything on earth has been altered while horseshoe crabs churned along apparently changelessly, skirting ice ages and outliving geologic catastrophies. In all the scrambling of geography, nature split the horseshoe crab population into two sections, one ranging the Atlantic Coast from Mexico to Maine and the other living not on the American Pacific Coast but along the coasts of Southeast Asia.

While many aristocrats consider themselves bluebloods, and although the horseshoe crab probably gives little thought to status, it is literally a blue-blooded animal. Man and other mammals have red blood because iron (in haemoglobin) is used in conveying oxygen in the blood stream. The horseshoe crab like crustacea and most mollusks has copper (in haemocyanin) instead of iron in its blood. Horseshoe crab blood turns blue when exposed to oxygen.

But blood color is only one of many curious differences between horseshoe crabs and even its closest relatives. After all, it isn't every creature that uses its legs to grind its food, can't eat without walking and has a mouth located near what we consider the center of our chest!

As with nearly all arthropods, growth occurs by molting, the animal escaping from its exoskeleton through a slit that develops around the front and side margins of the large shield-shaped part of its body. After the horseshoe crab has completely squeezed forward from its shell, the old shell virtually closes up and looks essentially like a living animal. Completely grown females are about 2 inches long; the males are always shorter. It is thought that the males do not molt after becoming mature. The eggs, larvae and adults are quite hardy and can be shipped alive for long distances. This and the fact that adults can survive for weeks without food and without water (if their gills are moist) has made these animals particularly valuable to the experimental invertebrate zoologist.

The horseshoe crab has crushing teeth in the form of short, closely-set spines located on the large upper joints of each of its five pairs of legs. As it travels along the ocean floor, with the rim of its shell shoved under the mud, bulldozing like a snowplow, the ten leg bases push together and grind small mollusks, algae, worms and other organisms gathered with the front pinchers. After grinding, the toothed basal leg sections pass this masticated material into the mouth located near the center of the undersurface between the third and fifth pair of

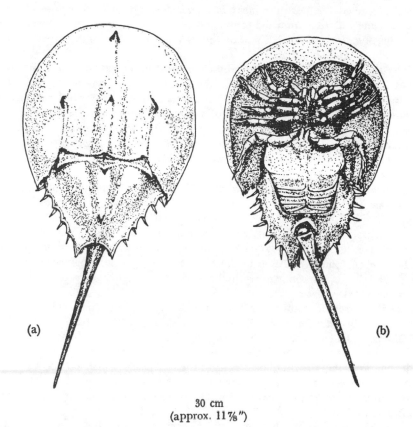

(a)   (b)

30 cm
(approx. 11⅞")

Limulus polyphemus—The Horseshoe or King Crab. (a) Dorsal. (b) Ventral. This ancient relative of the spider (it is not a crustacean) lives in shallow water along the shore where it burrows in the sand and mud and eats worms and other small animals.

legs. The whole operation is somewhat analagous to the movements of an automatic piece of machinery in that the animal cannot eat unless it is moving.

The long spine-like tail or telson may be moved in any direction because of its ball and socket type of attachment to the abdomen. It is used chiefly as a lever to help the animal right itself whenever it gets turned on to its back. The horseshoe-shaped shield protects it from other animals, and because its flange is kept embedded in the sand it keeps the animal from being upset by the waves. Progression is by a combination of walking and lurching: the four pairs of similar legs lift the body from the ground while the fifth pair, larger than the rest and ending in oddly constructed "pushers" that keep them from penetrating the sand but at the same time provide purchase, gives the body a violent shove forward. The fifth pair of legs, the telson, the hinged abdomen and the moveable spines along the sides of the abdomen act together in clearing away the sand, silt and mud during burrowing. This activity is amazingly rapid for an animal that seems basically awkward and clumsy.

Along the outside of each of two prominent lateral ridges on the back of the shield is a fairly large eye. In addition two small eyes are farther forward, one on each side of the less prominent median ridge. The basic structure of these eyes is quite different from the compound eyes of insects and crustaceans. A recent investigation revealed that *Limulus* is able to orient with respect to the plane of polarization of light.

The horseshoe crab differs radically from the true crabs. For one thing, true crabs have eyes on stalks while the horseshoe's eyes are set in the head. For another, the unique respiratory apparatus attached to the ventral side of the abdomen consisting of six pairs of gill-books differs radically from the gills of a shrimp or a lobster and are to be compared with the swimming appendages beneath the abdomen or tails of these animals. On the dissecting table, the horseshoe crab, after being separated from his distinctive shell, looks more like a scorpion then any other known living animal.

Through the years, scientists have argued about the classification of the horseshoe crab. For a century it was lumped together with such crustaceans as crabs and lobsters. However, in 1829, a German scientist pointed out that *Limulus*, (some zoologists insist that its scientific name is *Xiphosura*), was in no way similar to other crabs. He argued—as many still do today—that nothing alive today is even remotely related to the horseshoe crab. Now it has been assigned to the arachnids, in company with the spiders, mites, ticks, scorpions, harvest-men, and similar beasts.

Female horseshoe crabs deposit about 1000 eggs in each nest. They may return to the beach as many as 10 times in the spring, laying a total of more than 10,000 eggs. The nest is chosen apparently haphazardly. The female scuffs out a hollow in the sand, deposits the eggs usually at or just below the mean high tide line and the clinging smaller male then deposits sperm on top of them. The mass of eggs is quickly covered with sand and the area is smoothed by waves from the next tide. Ordinarily the laying season begins late in May and continues to July.

The tiny leathery-capsuled eggs—12 of them measure about an inch—hatch in July or August. The miniature horseshoe crabs crawl out of the sand and head immediately for the shallows where they may be found on sand or mud flats exposed at low tide. They are replicas of the parents but lack the spike tail and are known as "trilobite" larvae because of their close but superficial resemblance to these extinct crustacea.

Commonly the adults harbor a number of accidental associates, such as barnacles and slipper shells that may settle nearly anywhere on the upper or lower surfaces of the large anterior horseshoe-shaped part of the animal. More intimate associations are formed by ectocommensals such as the large cafe-au-lait-colored flatworm, (Turbellaria), *Bdelloura,* that lives between the book gills, using the cuticle of these organs as a substratum (basis for chemical action).

Where they have been collected in large numbers, horseshoe crabs have been used extensively as fertilizer on farms particularly along the northern part of the Atlantic Coast. In general, they are not known to gourmets, although the musculature is an esteemed delicacy in certain areas of the Middle Atlantic states.

Dollars in the Sand

The flat, thin, nearly circular skeletons of the rather curious group of echinoderms, sometimes encountered between tidelines by the itinerant stroller of the outer marine beaches, are commonly known as sand dollars. The name has been acquired because of their fancied resemblance of that fast-disappearing American coin, the silver dollar. They belong to the phylum Echinodermata, from the Greek words for hedgehog and skin, indicating that these are "spiny-skinned" animals. This division of animals contains the closely related sea stars, brittle stars, sea urchins, sea cucumbers and the ancient sea lilies.

The Echinodermata have skeletons constructed of calcareous plates with spines that are more or less embedded in the skin: in sea cucumbers, these are loosely scattered and the body is flexible; in sea stars and brittle stars, the plates articulate and the skeleton is somewhat pliable; whereas in sea urchins and sand dollars, the plates are fused and sutured together forming a box-like, immovable protective shell or test.

One of the most distinctive characteristics of echinoderms is that they all have radial symmetry (planes passed through the mouth or oral region will divide the animal into radial sectors) compared with the bi-lateral type of symmetry (lengthwise or vertical planes will divide the individual into equal and opposite right and left halves) commonly encountered in other metazoans including ourselves. This design is especially well demonstrated in sand dollars where the upper (aboral) surface has a starlike pattern of five petal-like figures radiating from a central disk-shaped sieve plate (the madreporite), the entrance to the unique locomotory vascular system. These petal-shaped regions on the aboral surface are the areas perforated by the animal's respiratory appartus. The underside (oral surface) has five relatively prominent equidistant channels (the ambulacral grooves) emanating from the central mouth. These grooves unite with similar less well defined structures on the upper surface and serve to pass strings of mucus containing food particles toward the mouth. The anal opening is at the edge of the test.

The northern sand dollar, *Echinarachnius parma,* ranging from mean low water to about 80 fathoms, from Long Island Sound northward, is about three inches in diameter and has no openings in its test, whereas the slightly larger southern sand dollar, or keyhole-urchin, *Mellita quinquiesperforata,* which is normally found from Cape Hatteras to the West Indies, but occasionally strays as far north as Martha's Vineyard, has its skeleton pierced by five elongate regularly spaced holes. The genus *Mellita* was originally described by the great naturalist, Louis Agassiz.

Living sand dolars are often abundant on sandy bottoms. Their tests are covered with a coating of large numbers of velvety fine spines that contrast with the long sturdy pointed spines of the closely related purple and green sea urchins. Both the tests and the spines vary from uniform light brown to purplish brown. Sand dollars live just below the surface of the sand. When exposed, they bury themselves by piling sand in front of them and moving into it. When the sand dollars die and are washed up on the beach, the spines fall off and the tests will eventually bleach and become white. When a test from a dead dollar

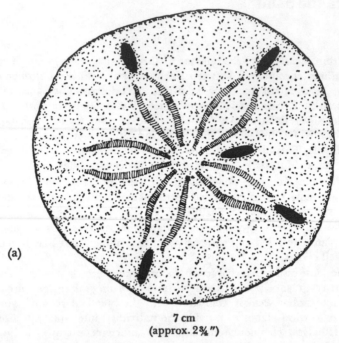

7 cm
(approx. 2¾″)

Sand Dollars. (a) *Mellita quinquiesperforata*—The Keyhole-urchin, common in south-ern shallow Atlantic waters, upper side.

is picked up and shaken, it rattles. The noise results from the now loosened and dried complicated dentary apparatus, called the Aristotle's lantern because of its fancied resemblance to an old Greek oil lamp. Aristotle's lantern in the living animal is an intricate and beautiful structure composed of five groups of calcareous plates bound by muscles from which five calcium carbonate teeth project to the outside. The teeth are used in obtaining the many small worms and other organisms on which these animals live.

Sand dollars move by the hydraulic tubefoot system, similar to the method used by starfish and sea urchins. Locomotion is the result of coordinated spine movements. In this system, water enters the water-vascular system through minute pores in the sieve plate, goes through a series of canals, and finally en-ters a hollow contractile bulb at the inner end of each tube foot. When the bulb contracts the tube lengthens, and when it is relaxed the tube is with-drawn. The ends of the tube feet are sucking disks. Since the action of all the tube feet is coordinated, they work together to pull the animal along.

In sand dollars, the sexes are separate; eggs and sperm are spawned directly into the surrounding water through the five small openings around the sieve plate. After fertilization, development into free-swimming planktonic ciliated bilaterally symmetrical larvae takes place, and several weeks later the larvae metamorphose into radially symmetrical adults and settle to the bottom. This is one of the most remarkable metamorphoses in the animal kingdom. Only a small percentage survive since most of the larvae become lost, are eaten, or settle in the wrong environment. The eggs of sand dollars have been a favorite tool of

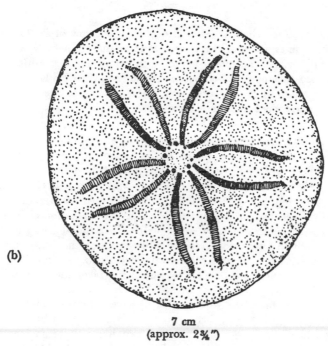

7 cm
(approx. 2¾")

(b) *Echinarachnius parma*—The Sand Dollar, common from Long Island Sound northward. Upper (aboral) side.

experimental embryologists since the first decades of this century. The reasons for the active interest of these biologists in the reproductive products of echinoids lies in their relative availability, hardiness, facility of culture in the laboratory, and their readily observable habits of growth and development.

Apparently, starfishes are one of the main enemies of sand dollars. When a starfish crosses a bed of sand dollars, it has been observed that the dollars down current from the starfish quickly bury themselves. It has been reported reliably that flounders, cod and haddock feed extensively on sand dollars when occasion arises.

Through the ages, the sand dollar has been used as both ornament and amulet. In some quarters these animals are known as the Holy Ghost shell because the markings on the shell symbolize the birth and crucifixion and resurrection of Christ. The five-pointed star on the underside of the sand dollar represents the Star of Bethlehem, and also resembles the outline of an Easter lily. The narrow elliptical openings are reminiscent of the five wounds made in the body of Christ during crucifixion. On the underside of the shell is an easily recognized outline of the Christmas poinsettia. When the shell is broken open, cells are found each holding five objects that look like five birds in flight. These represent the doves of peace. Another interpretation of these bird-like objects connects them to the angels who sang to the shepherds on the first Christmas morning.

The Native Sea Cucumbers

Strewn on and buried slightly below the muddy bottoms of shallow embayments bordering the estuaries of the coastal zone of the southern New England states is the rough-coated *Thyone briareus,* member of a rather curious group of animals, the sea cucumbers. These animals belong to the class Holothuroidea, a representative group of the radially symmetrical phylum of five-parted, spiny-skinned invertebrates, the Echinodermata.

More widely spread and always found in burrows in firm sand or mud in many local subtidal flats is the related genus *Leptosynapta,* often mistaken for a member of one of the groups of worms because of its elongate vermiform shape. There are two species of this animal in our coastal waters: *Leptosynapta inhaerens,* a pale gray creature, and *Leptosynapta roseola,* a roseate beast. The leptosynaptid cucumbers may be easily separated from the worms by noting the five branching tentacles at their anterior ends (almost entirely contractable), the five faint white stripes that run the length of their bodies, and the clinging sensation received when running the fingers along the outside of the body. If the tentacles are contracted when the animal is found, it can be put into a quiet body of sea water until it relaxes and these structures appear.

At first glance, sea cucumbers would seem to have little resemblance to such other echinoderms as sea urchins, brittle stars, starfishes and sea biscuits; nevertheless, they all have the same basic five part (pentamerous) arrangement. Perhaps the easiest way to note this pattern is to hold the animal vertically and look directly down at it toward the end with the tentacles. Another way to think about sea cucumbers being echinoderms is to view them as disk-shaped starfish that have grown into the shape of a shopping bag pointed at one end and slightly truncated at the other.

Holothuroideans use the tentacles for feeding, the mouth being in the center of the crown of tentacles. The tentacles are covered with a fairly sticky mucoid material to which living and non-living particles adhere. After a tentacle is covered with material it is put into the mouth, and whatever has stuck to it is scraped off. Food consists almost entirely of microscopic fauna and flora, detritus and one-celled plants collected as the waving tentacles sweep through the water or along the surface of the sand or mud substrate. Since all three of the local sea cucumbers often live below the surface of the bottom (*Leptosynapta* is characteristically a burrower and *Tyhone* may excavate a U-shaped burrow), they may swallow a great deal of sand, much in the manner of an earthworm. The material in which they are burrowing is passed through their bodies and the nutritive substances are digested out.

Thus the holothuroideans have become the only really successful burrowing forms among the echinoderms, a living habit that has probably been brought about by their armless condition and sausage shape, and by their possession of a muscular body wall with small, widely separated calcium carbonate skeletal elements. In the other echinoderms, these calcium carbornate ossicles are more numerous and closer together, resulting in the formation of a more or less rigid skeleton.

10 cm
(approx. 4")

Thyone briareus—The New England Cucumber.

Although sea cucumbers may be relatively insensitive to light, they have a well-developed sense of touch. This serves them as a means of protection. The worm-shaped leptosynaptids contract sharply and may break into two or more pieces when mechanically disturbed or roughly handled. The more conventionally shaped globose forms react to this kind of stimulus by contracting the body and rupturing the cloaca with subsequent expulsion of the respiratory trees, the digestive tract and the gonads. In *Thyone,* the anterior end ruptures with consequent expelling of the tentacles, pharynx, part of the intestine and associated organs. This violent reaction is not often fatal since most species of holothurians have great powers of regeneration, and the lost organs are soon replaced. In *Thyone,* the cloacal region (aboral, the end opposite the tentacles) is the center of regeneration. Great regenerative power in sea cucumbers should not be surprising since other echinoderms such as the common starfish can replace entire lost arms.

Synaptids respire through the general body surface. However, in *Thyone* and its close relatives there is a unique and remarkable system of tubules called respiratory trees, one on each side of the digestive tract. The trunks of the two trees arise from the cloaca, and it is by means of the pumping action of the cloaca that water is forced in and out of the respiratory trees. In this way, new water is constantly gulped in through the anus and oxygen is brought to various parts of the body.

Sea cucumbers ordinarily move around by means of pentamerous rows of tube feet. However, all three of the local holothuroideans provide exceptions.

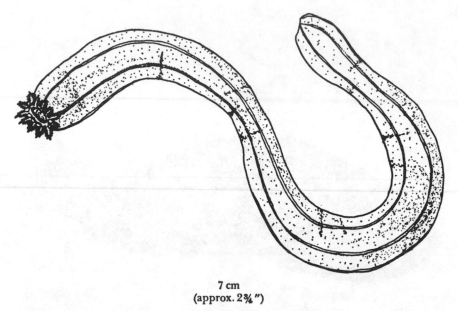

7 cm
(approx. 2¾")

Leptosynapta inhaerens—The Glass Worm, an elongate, translucent holothurian or sea cucumber.

Thyone has podia (feet) on both surfaces of the body with suckers best developed on the podia of the sole; they creep about slowly. *Leptosynapta* lack tube feet altogether and move about by using tentacles as holdfasts. These animals push into the sand with alternate contractions of their circular and longitudinal muscles, pushing the sand aside with their tentacles, moving at a rate of two to three centimeters an hour. Young leptosynaptids are able to swim by lashing out both ends of the body at the same time while they are temporarily U-shaped.

Reproduction in holothurians is much the same as in other echinoderms, except that even the hermaphroditic members of this class have only a single gonad. The eggs of relatives of both the local *Thyone* and *Leptosynapta* undergo incubation in which the eggs pass through the gonads into the body cavity and are fertilized. Here they are brooded while developing, the young eventually leaving the mother's body by means of a break near the anus and becoming members of the zooplankton.

Although none of the local holothurians has been used as food, a large warmwater form *(Stichopus)* has a more glutinous and less leathery body wall and is highly prized by the Chinese. The Chinese are said to relish a meal of "trepang," which consists of sun-dried body walls of several species of *Holothuria*, *Stichopus*, and *Thelenota*. "It is employed," says Edward Forbes, "in the preparation of nutritious soups, in common with an esculent seaweed, sharks' fins, edible birds' nests . . . affording much jelly." Holothurians may also come to the table as Bechê-de-Mer.

The Sea Urchin And Its Life

The sea urchin often found in the tide pools and along some of the rock-strewn shores south of the lower Cape (Cape Cod), is a curious, slow-moving reddish to dark purplish, hemispherical spine-covered animal known to the zoologist as *Arbacia punctulata*. It belongs to the same group of organisms as the starfish, sand dollars and sea lilies, a phylum of radially symmetrical, pentamerous (body divisions and many internal structures occurring in fives or multiples of five) ancient beasts, the echinoderms or spiny-skinned animals, found in nearly all of the seas on earth.

Arbacia lives along the eastern coast of North America from Woods Hole, Martha's Vineyard and Nantucket to Florida often intertidally, but more frequently in depths of from 20 to 90 feet and on down to about 700 feet. They are more often found in large, widely separated groups or "beds" of variously sized animals rather than as individuals going it alone. The shells or tests of commonly found individuals (measured without the spines) vary from ¼ to 2¼ inches in diameter and from ⅛ to 1½ inches in height, and are generally about half as high as they are wide. The conical sharply pointed but non-poisonous spines, shortest and relatively flat at the base are longest along the sides, averaging about 1½ inches in this area.

Because the sea urchin is radially symmetrical instead of bilaterally symmetrical like ourselves it has an oral (mouth) and an aboral surface rather than the dorsal and ventral surfaces of vertebrates. The oral surface with its central mouth is the flattened area of the animal, while the aboral surface is punctured at the peak of the dome by a small anus.

Dead sea urchins quickly lose their muscle-attached spines and when washed up on the beach exhibit a unique pentamerous arrangement of variously punctured and sculptured plates tightly fitted together like the pieces in a newly constructed jigsaw puzzle. The total number of plates varies with the size of the individual. The large heart-shaped madreporic plate on the aboral surface is like a sieve through whose microscopic holes water enters. The water drawn in through this organ is vital in the operation of the ambulacral (water walking) system, an organ system found only in echinoderms. Through each of the holes in the lateral plates of the living animal extends a long slender tube foot ending on a water-operated suction cup. Above the small rounded knobs on these same plates the spines articulate closely by means of their cup-shaped bases. Between the spines are two- or three-jointed jaw-like pedicellaria that wave back and forth snatching foreign objects from the surface of the sea urchin.

When an intact, dried *Arbacia* shell or test is shaken it makes a rattling noise. This is caused by a rather large and complexly structured dental apparatus called "Aristotle's Lantern" because its original description by Aristotle caused later zoologists to mark its resemblance to antique Greek lanterns of the same period.

The sea urchin may move in any direction, using its spines and tube feet to travel at a rate of about one inch per minute. When placed on its aboral surface in water, *Arbacia* uses these same structures to turn itself over to its normal

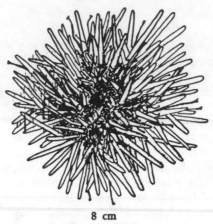

8 cm
(approx. 3⅛")

Arbacia punctulata—The Purple Sea Urchin.

position. Ordinarily, in shallow environments sea urchins tend to move away from the light and are found in shaded or darker areas, often in empty bivalve shells or under overhanging rocks.

In collecting *Arbacia,* the best place to look is along rocks or shelly bottoms. The scuba diver can pick them up easily by hand while the collector in a boat must drag a starfish "mop" over the bottom to which the sea urchins cling by their pedicellaria until they are brought on board.

Arbacia can regenerate spines, tube feet, pedicellaria and if undisturbed they can heal shell fractures. They live well in the ordinary saltwater aquarium and can go without eating for more than a month at a time, apparently without ill effect. However they are omnivorous, eating a great variety of living material including rockweed, sea lettuce, coral, sponges, mussels, sand dollars, other *Arbacia,* live and dead fish, etc.

Great quantities of *Arbacia* have been used since the turn of the century by experimental embryologists in studying various phases of growth and development. For this reason much is known about the life history of these animals from the shedding of eggs and sperm, through the planktonic larval stages to the metamorphosed adult. It is interesting that in spite of the tremendous amount of investigation on these animals, zoologists are still unable to tell the sexes apart!

Although sea urchins have been used as food by man from time immemorial, it is a larger species such as the green sea urchin, *Strongylocentrotus drobachiensis,* from the coast of Maine, whose gonads particularly the eggs, are highly regarded by gourmets. *Arbacia* is eaten in turn by many kinds of fish such as cod and haddock, as well as starfish, spider crabs, and fellow *Arbacia.* Long before the time of Pliny, both raw and cooked sea urchins were used as medicine for a variety of ills including as an antidote for certain poisonous plants. Not only have the shells or tests been used in various places at different times as cups, flower pots and even lamps but they have been found as part of the motif in decorations on ancient vases, coins and jewelry.

70

Star of the Sea

The common sea star or starfish as it is often called, lives in the waters of the western Atlantic Coast from Maine to the Gulf of Mexico, but it is relatively rare north of Massachusetts where it overlaps the range of the common Northern Starfish or Purple Star, *Asterias vulgaris*. In the main it is a shallow water form although it has been found in more than 500 fathoms of water. The best time to beach-comb for it is during low tide when individuals may be found lurking in the dark corners, crevices and crannies of tide pools, under or along the sides of rocks and empty shells, or concentrated near collections of live snails or bivalves. Sea stars may be colored from light orange through a variety of shades of dark purple or greenish-black. Supposedly there are two kinds of sea stars in mid-New England (Massachusetts and Rhode Island) waters, *Asterias forbesi* (named after the famous Scotch zoologist, Edward Forbes): an animal with stout, blunt cylindrical arms, scattered spines and a bright orange madreporite (a sieve plate through which water enters the ambulacral system) and *Asterias vulgaris* with flattened, pointed arms or rays, numerous spines that seem to form a single obvious median line on each arm and a pale yellow madreporite. However, so many local sea stars have been found intermediate in character between these two species that a number of zoologists now feel that there is actually only a single species.

Sea stars were well known to Aristotle and his contemporaries and one finds interesting and sometimes startling accounts of them in the writings of several medieval naturalists. However, it was not until 1733 when Johannes Linck, a German zoologist and physician from Leipzig, described their anatomy, that our present knowledge of the group started.

Normally these echinoderms have bodies with the form of a five-rayed star, but some individuals, because of autotomy (the ability to cast off a part of the body) and an abnormality of subsequent regeneration, may be found with six, seven, eight or even nine arms. Animals with less than five arms or with arms shorter than others either have not started to regenerate or have not finished the year necessary to complete new growth.

As is the case with all echinoderms, sea stars are radially symmetrical with spicules or plates of calcium carbonate in the body wall forming an internal skeleton, and a system of fluid-carrying tubes and canals extending throughout the body called a water-vascular or ambulacral system because of its use in locomotion. Sea stars are usually oriented with the surface on which the mouth is located (oral surface) downwards or against the substratum. If a living sea star is turned over, the membranous area surrounding the mouth (the peristome) is easily seen. From this structure and extending along the midline of each arm is a deep groove from which tube-feet in four rows wave in all directions. After replacing the animal on its oral surface the general shape of the central disk with its eccentric and often brilliantly colored circular madreporite and its five radiating arms covered with a mixture of three types of short spines or tubercles immediately becomes obvious. A hand lens is necessary to see the small anal opening near the center of the disk, the very small jaw-like, (sometimes extensible) pedicelariae distributed over the surface and used to keep this

12 cm
(approx. 4¾")

Asterias forbesi—The Common Starfish.

area free of detritus, the minute finger-like fleshy growths around the base of the spines with which respiration is accomplished, and the pink to red eye-spot at the tip of each arm surrounded by very small tentacles shaped like common pins. The entire surface of the body is ciliated.

Although the sexes in sea stars are separate, it is nearly impossible to tell the difference between males and females externally except when the latter's arms are plump and relatively soft, filled with the large orange eggs. Fertilization of the eggs takes place after the sexual products are shed freely into the salt water. In a short while they develop into a bilaterally symmetrical larva called a bipinnaria. Breeding season is in the spring; the number of eggs shed depends on the size of the sea star, a 9- to 12-inch female shedding as many as

2,500,000 eggs. Eventually the bipinnaria larva goes through several additional stages before it undergoes one of the most remarkable changes in the animal kingdom by metamorphosing into a radially symmetrical, easily recognizable sea star less than 1 millimeter in diameter, and settling to the bottom.

The size of sea stars depends directly on the amount of food eaten and not on chronological age. Research has revealed the rather curious facts that in winter the ossicles making up the skeleton shrink together, reducing the overall size of the animals, and that also at this time of year the animals migrate in relatively large groups from shallow to deeper waters. Divers and underwater photography have revealed that sea stars not only move by means of their tube feet, but that they may also be transported passively just above the bottom by tidal currents. These observations explain their unexpected and rapid appearance in large numbers on ground previously unsettled.

The sea star is a carnivore and is economically important for its highly destructive predation on all of the edible mollusks and crustacea (barnacles) it can reach. The list includes the more familiar commercial species such as oysters, quahogs, mussels, periwinkles as well as limpets, cockles, and a variety of snails and scallops, when they can be caught. Prescise statistics for sea star predation are not available but a few examples suffice to indicate its power: in 1887, Connecticut estimated that it lost 634,246 bushels of oysters worth $463,000 to these animals; again in 1929 one oyster company removed more than 10 million set stars from 11,000 acres of oyster grounds in Narragansett Bay. A 1961 starfish survey showed that they reached a density of 1000-2000 per 2000 square yards in three regions of Narragansett Bay.

Sea stars are collected from the bay bottom by dredging or by dragging enlarged versions of the kitchen wetmop over starfish beds. The animals cling to the mops with the pedicellariae and are brought to the decks of the collecting vessels. Before their powers of regeneration were recognized the method of disposal was to tear them in pieces and toss them overboard, however today they are more profitably heaped, dried and ground into fertilizer or included in poultry feed.

It seems somewhat strange that in spite of many documented observations over the years the answer to the question of how the sea star opens its prey has not been settled to the satisfaction of invertebrate zoologists. Certainly these animals leave no marks on their victims! Apparently, a sea star settles on a bivalve with its central disk close to the hinge of its prey, two of its arms spread on one shell and three arranged on the opposite valve. By pulling the shells in opposite directions with tube feet exerting a force in excess of 6 lbs. per square inch a tiny crack is made less than $\frac{1}{32}$ inch wide through which narcotizing fluid from the sea star's stomach may or may not be injected. In any case, the opening is sufficiently large for insertion of the everted stomach of the sea star. The soft parts of the live mollusk are quickly digested, the stomach is drawn back inside the predator's body from the now empty shells of its prey and the sea star moves onward in search of its next victim.

New England's Most Primitive
Living Marine Mollusk

Along the rocky groins of the harbors and in among the tide pools formed by cobbles and boulders live biologically interesting members of the most primitive class of mollusks that inhabit these shallow waters. These animals, commonly known as chitons (from the Greek word for tunic or coat of mail), and nearly worldwide in distribution, belong to the class Amphineura, and to the order Polyplacophora. *Chaetopleura apiculata*, common along the entire east coast from Cape Cod to Florida, is considered to be the most successful of the molluscan minor groups.

Similar to its close relatives, *Tonicella marmorea* and *Ischnocheton ruber* that range in deep waters from Long Island Sound northward and become circumpolar, the more southerly *Chaetopleura* are greatly flattened mollusks, with a rudimentary head that differs from the heads of most snails (Gastropoda) in having neither tentacles nor eyes. The feature that readily distinguishes chitons from other mollusks is the shell of eight slightly overlapping plates or valves arranged in a longitudinal row covering the dorsal (top) surface of the animal. This shell, secreted by the underlying mantle, is surrounded by a girdle (part of the mantle) whose ornamentation is readily revealed by the microscope. The sculpturing of the shell has a practical aspect as far as the chiton is concerned since, in most cases, it is caused by very small canals associated with sense organs called aesthetes.

In *Chaetopleura*, the girdle surrounding the plates is hairy and the plates are gray or yellowish, sometimes with a reddish tinge. An obvious keel runs along the center of each of the plates, the plates in turn being covered irregularly with small tubercles. Adult chaetopleurans are commonly found from Cape Cod to Florida.

The ventral (bottom) surface of chitons is nearly all foot; it is typically broad and flat, and is used to adhere to shells or to a rocky substrate. Propulsion is accomplished entirely by muscular waves along the sole of the foot. When a strenuous attempt is made to detach these animals, the girdle is forcibly applied against the rock and the foot is retracted. This reaction enables the ventral surface to form a powerful suction cup and makes removal of the animal quite difficult. For this reason, chitons, by and large, are found on smooth rocks and shells because of the better adhesion provided by a smooth surface. If one is sufficiently fortunate to loosen its hold, it rolls into a ball much like a pill bug or a sow bug when it is picked up, the dorsal valves forming a protective covering or shield.

Spawning in chitons usually shows some degree of lunar periodicity. Although the sexes are separate, it is virtually impossible to differentiate visibly the males from the females. The females do not shed their ova until the males have released their sperm into the surrounding water, but exactly what causes the male to start this course of events is not known. One hypothesis for the start of male sperm release holds that this reaction is a response to a chemical stimulus from the female. In any case, it is quite fortunate that chitons are generally gregarious since grouping enables at least some sperm to reach the females and

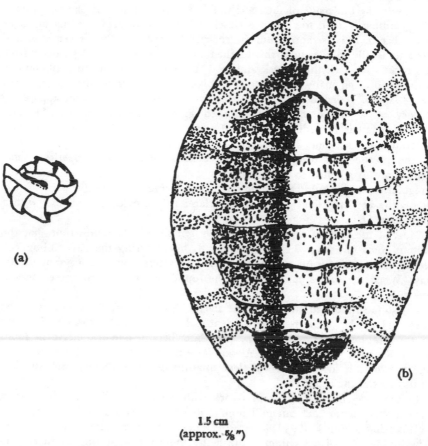

(a)

(b)

1.5 cm
(approx. ⅝″)

Chaetopleura apiculata—The Common Eastern Chiton. (a) When disturbed, the chiton curls up like a pill bug. (b) Clearly shows the dorsal armature of 8 transverse calcareous plates.

fertilize the ova inside the mantle cavity. The eggs are shed into the sea in masses or strings. Fertilized eggs soon develop into a planktonic (floating) larva that metamorphoses directly into a bottom-living juvenile, a small edition of its parents.

Most of the 600 known species of chitons are inconspicuously colored, their dull shades of red, brown, yellow or green blending into their rock-strewn background and providing excellent protection from their enemies. Nearly all chitons are under three inches long. *Chaetopleura* is drab in color and grows to a length of about three quarters of an inch. The largest forms have been collected on the Pacific Coast, *Katherinia* and *Ischnochiton* reaching a length of about 12 inches. Although these animals have been found to a depth of 12,000 feet, *Chaetopleura*, like most other chitons worldwide, lives in shallow, barely subtidal waters in areas where the bottom is lined with rocks and sometimes shells.

Unlike many other mollusks chitons, wander very little unless they are disturbed. If a rock bearing a chiton is turned over, the chiton will slowly make its way to the underside of the rock; this is a good example of photonegativity. They ordinarily tend to stay in a closely circumscribed area, feeding on algae and other material scraped from the rocky substrate with their seven jaws and their unusually long radula; this toothed structure scrapes small particles from the rocks with a rhythmic back and forth motion. The radula is a ribbon-like structure bearing many transverse rows of 17 teeth per row, the central teeth being largest. It has been observed that when a subradular organ, apparently sensory or a chemoreceptor, is applied against the substratum, the subradular organ is immediately retracted and replaced by the radula after food is located. On occasion, individuals may go on a short scouting trip, returning to the precise spot they started from, after satisfying their appetites. Some chitons are so adapted to one location that their girdle becomes shaped to the irregularities of the substrate, while other species find and then live permanently in cavities or depressions in the rock surfaces that provide their bodies with a fairly close fit.

Most of the feeding activities occur at night since it is at this time that the chitons come out from the dark places inhabited during the day. Chiton collecting is most successful out on the rocks or in tide pools on foggy or cloudy days. When the sun is out, they must be found by turning over loose rocks at low tide.

It was the American Indians of the Pacific Northwest and the natives of the West Indies who discovered independently the virtues and pleasures of dining on the local large species of chitons. They later became one of the favorite foods of the Russians who first settled Alaska. The chitons of our coast are too small and too difficult to collect in sufficient quantity to make them a common dish in this part of the country.

Chitons may be removed from a rock with a sudden well directed, sideways blow before the animal can pull itself tightly to the substrate, or failing this, by inserting a thin knife blade between rock and the animal's muscular foot. The edible part of the chiton is the fleshy foot, and according to those who have tried it, it is delicious raw, with or without lemon juice or cocktail sauce. In the West Indies, chiton meat is known as "sea beef." It may be fried or boiled, and is used in soups and chowders.

Jingle Shells, the Beachcomber's Delight

The very handsome, slightly convex oval shells with a yellow or golden mother-of-pearl sheen, often found high up on exposed marine beaches, are the so-called "jingle shells," also known as "mermaid's toenails," an obvious reference to their general shape. The outer surface of living "jingles" is scaly and dark colored, sometimes covered with what appear to be groups of prickly radiating lines. When the animals die, this rough covering is usually worn off, exposing the silvery or translucent shades underneath.

The two species of jingle shells in New England waters are the small *Anomia aculeata* whose irregularly rounded and moderately fragile shell is no more than about 25 millimeters (about one inch) in diameter, and the more common and larger *Anomia simplex*, an animal with a thin but strong shell, ordinarily twice the size of *Anomia aculeata*. Both mollusks have been known for a long time, the larger of the two having appeared in the tenth edition of *The Systema Naturae* (1758), by the famous Carolus Linnaeus. While *Anomia aculeata* ranges from Long Island to the Arctic Ocean, it is most common attached to rocks and broken shells in waters north of Cape Cod from 1 to 80 fathoms. It is also found in Europe. *Anomia simplex* has been collected from Nova Scotia southward around the Florida peninsula to Texas; and it occurs in the West Indies and in Europe. In all these areas it lives in shallow sublittoral waters and is especially abundant on oyster beds, logs, wharves and sometimes even on boats. Individuals that have become buried in the mud are blackened; however, normal coloration can be restored by exposure to free-flowing seawater. Although the jingle is eaten in Europe, we in this country apparently have not yet discovered how delicious this bivalve really is.

The jingle shells belong in the family *Anomiidae*, one of about a dozen other families of the order *Filibranchia* that include such more or less commonly found shellfish as oysters, scallops, pearl oysters, kitten paws, mussels and the ark shells or cockles. The generic name, *Anomia*, is derived from the Greek "anomos" meaning irregular or uneven, and undoubtedly refers to the uneven size or asymmetry of the two shells. The upper or free valve is usually quite convex, whereas the much smaller lower valve is flattened and has a hole near its apex or hinge end. The lower shell is molded and cemented so firmly to whatever it is fastened on that it never breaks free, consequently it is only the top shells of the animals that are washed ashore whenever there is sufficient disturbance to the substrate of living or dead jingles to cause the shells to part company.

Unlike the oyster, the jingle fastens itself to rocks or other substrata by its right or lower valve. It is through the nearly circular hole or deep embayment in this flat shell that the calcified band of byssus is extended to fix the animal to a permanent resting place for the remainder of its life. It will be remembered that the byssus is a special gland in the foot of filibranchians that secretes tough viscous threads which are first attached when the foot is extended and pressed against the substrate. Then, as this organ retracts from the substrate, the threads are spun out. The byssus threads coalesce into a cable which hardens and calcifies on contact with water. Byssal retractor muscles are at-

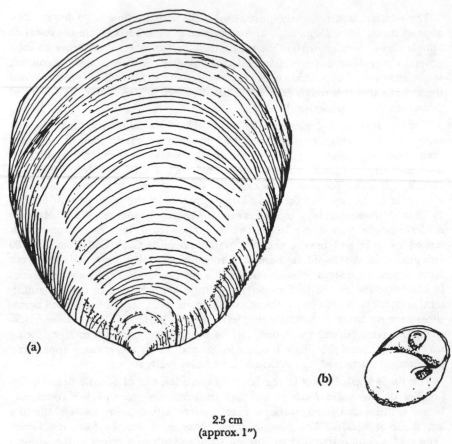

(a)

(b)

2.5 cm
(approx. 1″)

Crepidula plana—The Flat Slipper Shell. (a) **External view showing minute apex.**
(b) **Customary position adhering to interior of moon shell inhabited by a hermit
crab.**

tached from the bottom to the upper shell and serve, like the shell muscles of
the limpet, to pull the animal down against the substrate. This means that in
this animal (like the limpet) there is really only one functional valve, the
movable upper shell. In nature, the edge of the upper shell clamps down close
against the hard substrate.

Jingle shells lack siphons, a characteristic they share with scallops, but not
with clams. However, like all other bivalves, the jingles have ciliated gills. The
cilia are spread along the gill surface and are used to build a food-collecting
and a food-storing device. This mechanism operates by drawing small particles
and microscopic organisms over the gill surfaces where they are delivered and
concentrated in ciliated food grooves. The food grooves carry this material to
the small flaplike palps. Here the food is sorted, and the items of acceptable
size are conveyed to the mouth where they are ingested.

Both *Anomia simplex* and *Anomia aculeata* have been found in biologically interesting associations with other organisms. Both species are most often observed living in the same habitat, the larger one attached to oysters more than to any other organisms. A few years ago, a marine invertebrate zoologist at the Marine Biological Laboratory in Woods Hole was working on a marine polychaete, *Polydora*, a relative of the clam worm, which lives in shells of bay scallops. He found that the population of scallops with *Anomia simplex* attached by its calcified byssus threads had far lower numbers of *Polydora* than clean scallops, or scallops with other attached organisms. This indicated to him that the presence of *Anomia* on scallop shells exerted more or less exclusive influence in keeping *Polydora* away from scallops.

Children prefer jingle shells to many other kinds of shells easily collected on our beaches; jingles are usually plentiful, they are bright and pretty, they are easily used in a variety of handicrafts, and they rarely need to be cleaned or polished.

We collect the jingle shell so numerous
By means of ulna, radius and humerous,
And bring them to the creative dreamers
On tired tibias and fibulas and femurs!

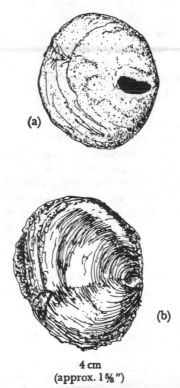

(a)

(b)

4 cm
(approx. 1⅝")

Anomia simplex—The Jingle Shell. (a) Flat lower shell with a hole through which the byssal threads attach the animal to rocks or other shells. (b) The upper valve of the shell.

A Local Snail That Harbors Bather's Itch

The eastern mud snail, *Ilyanassa obsoleta,* belongs to a group of gastropods often called dog whelks. It is without doubt the most commonly found snail on most of the mud flats of the bays and the salt ponds of New England. In tidal mud flats, it can often be seen in large numbers either collected in shallow depressions left by the receding tides or easing along just below the film of water covering the intervening mud surfaces. Characteristic trails often indicate the presence of the mud snail in undisturbed areas. In cold weather, motion is less rapid, for fewer snails are found along the surface, and greater concentrations are seen in the deeper pools.

The mud snail is a small dun-colored animal varying in shade from brown to black, an animal that blends well with its environment. Its conical shell has an elevated spire with six whorls and a surface weakly reticulated by many longitudinal and revolving striations that distinguish it from other snails living in the same area. The lowest whorl is larger than the rest. Very often the modest reticulations on the surface are obscured by microbial or diatom growth to which cling particles of mud that not only disguise the nature of the shell sculpturing, but also make the animal slippery to touch.

Adult animals are about an inch and one-quarter long and a half-inch across at the widest point. The opening in the largest whorl is oval and has a short notch at its base and a row of very small toothlike knobs just inside the outer lip. If the shell is held away from the light its purplish lining can be seen relatively easily. Living mud snails have a reddish brown horny operculum or "door" to the shell whose edges are quite smooth.

While gliding along the bottom, the two most obvious characteristics of the mud snail are the squareness of the front of the foot and the long tubular anterior canal slowly being pointed in first one direction and then in another in the apparently never-ending search for food. At the base of this spout is the unique file-like rasping organ or radula consisting of a ribbon with three longitudinal rows of teeth variously decorated with cusps. The constant back and forth motion of the radula wears away living or dead flesh, bringing the particles to the roof of the mouth where cilia take them to the esophagus. Here they are bound together with mucous and are carried in a viscous string through the remainder of the digestive tract, eventually being eliminated in the form of pellets. The number, size and character of the teeth and the type of fecal pellets are used in identification of snails.

Mud snails feed almost entirely on dead and decaying materials. Probably very helpful in this regard is the presence of an organ between the spout and the gills called an osphradium. This structure is analagous to the nose of man in terms of testing the quality of the environment for the presence of food. In mud snails it is thought that this organ can also help interpret the type of sediment on which the animal is gliding.

The mud snail occurs from the Gulf of the St. Lawrence River to Key West and north along the West Coast of Florida, being found in greatest numbers south of Cape Cod.

Mud snails drew a great deal of attention in Rhode Island some years ago

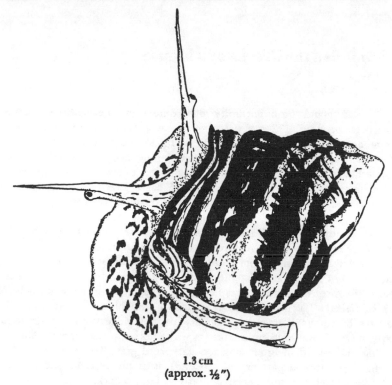

1.3 cm
(approx. ½")

Ilyanassa obsoleta—The Mud Snail.

when the Rhode Island Department of Health received many complaints from fishermen and bathers in several Narragansett Bay areas about a skin irritation apparently resulting from exposure to waters of the Bay.

Studies by the department indicated that it was the same kind of dermatitis produced in fresh water in this country and abroad by one of the intermediate stages (cercaria) of the life-cycle of a blood fluke of the genus *Schistosoma*. The infection was called "cercaria dermatitis" or bather's itch. It proved to be caused by an animal new to science which was given the name *Cercaria variglandis*. Malcolm Hinchliffe of the R.I. Department of Health and Horace Stunkard of the American Museum of Natural History determined its life history and biology.

It was determined that this blood-fluke normally lives in waterfowl and wading birds. When infested birds landed on mud flats and released the blood-fluke eggs in their droppings, the eggs hatched into microscopic ciliated forms that eventually found their way into the mud snails. There they developed into infective cercaria over the winter and were released by the snails when the water turned warmer in the spring at the same time that the waterfowl again stopped on their way north. The blood-fluke was attracted by the warm-blooded human swimmers but could not bore into the blood stream of this abnormal host and died in the thick skin, producing an infection.

Probably the most practical method of preventing bather's itch would be to decrease the population of mud snails by rehabilitating the mud flats. This may be accomplished most easily by reducing the amount of refuse and other wastes which now pollute them and on which a great many of the mud snails feed.

It Reminded the Greeks of a Mouse

In New England the opportunity to become a gourmet at little expense and effort is tremendous. The salt waters of the area harbor a great number of marine organisms that could and should be included in our diet.

One delicacy that the French discovered long ago is the edible mussel—a smooth-shelled blue to violet to blue-black three- to six-inch mollusk whose scientific name is *Mytilus edulis*. The mussel has a sweet, nut-like flavor which will appeal to those who object to the "fishy" taste of some shellfish.

Mussels grow in clusters of up to 500 on both exposed and unexposed areas of bays, ponds, inlets and rocky outcrops. Each sea mussel is anchored by a "byssus" or beard to a stone, rock piling or similar substratum.

It is possible to confuse the edible sea mussel with species of horse mussels which are not nearly as palatable, and which it resembles closely. There are three easily discernible differences between sea mussels and horse mussels (*Modiolus modiolus*): (1) the sea mussel is smooth and blue-black in color whereas the dark brown horse mussel is ribbed with long ridges; (2) the sea mussel is nearly always found growing in clusters while horse mussels occur as individuals growing half-buried in intertidal mud flats, cord grass flats or mud banks; and (3) the beak (raised part or pointed end) is at the extreme end of the shell of the sea mussel, but in the horse mussel it is farther back.

The Greeks can be blamed for the name of the mussel, which is derived from the Greek word meaning mouse. The best guess is that the Greeks had in mind the fact that the dark shell of the mussel resembles the coat of a sleeping mouse.

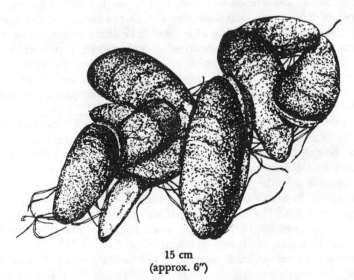

15 cm
(approx. 6")

Mytilus edulis—The Sea or Edible Mussel often lives in the most heavily populated part of the intertidal region among the plants low on a rocky shore with a large variety of both sessile and mobile invertebrates.

Oysters "R" for Eating

Let us royster with the oyster—in the shorter days and moister,
They are brought by brown September, with its roguish final "R";
For breakfast or for supper, on the under shell or upper,
Of dishes he's the daisy, and of shell-fish he's the star.

The Detroit Free Press, October 12, 1889

There is probably no animal—certainly no mollusk—that has had so much written about it—all in a pleasurable vein—for the past two thousand years. It has been praised by gourmet and by gourmand, adulated by poet and playwright and has inspired the brushes of such artists as Van der Meer, Steen and Manet. Oysters have titillated the palates of mankind wherever and whenever eating became an art instead of a necessity.

For this reason, if for no other, the oyster has attracted the attention of zoologists who have sought methods of helping it grow and maintain itself in the face of the ever-increasing pressures of the marketplace.

Oysters are sessile organisms and have become greatly modified structurally in this sedentary way of life. There is a minute larval stage that becomes a part of the great body of marine zooplankton (the microscopic organisms that wander about at the mercy of wind, current and wave) until it settles on some hard object such as rock or shell fragment on the bottom. This small creature, now metamorphosed into a recognizable though minute bivalve, is cemented to substratum by its right valve or shell. During this change, the foot disappears and the gill extends around the entire rounded part of the animal between the shells. If the oyster has settled in a favorable environment it will reach commercial size, from three to four inches long, in from three to five years. Six-inch specimens are not uncommon, and 12- to 15-inch oysters have been found in waters off the New York and New England coasts. The oyster is virtually the only bivalve mollusk with unlike shells, and its shape depends on that of the object to which it is attached. Because of this, the very large, more or less convex oysters sold in New York City restaurants are known as "saddlebacks." On a menu, oysters usually are named for the place from which they came; thus "Cotuits" come from the south shore of Cape Cod, "Blue Points" come from Long Island Sound, and so on.

According to Paul Galtsoff, dean of American investigators on the biology of oysters, the environment itself may interfere with the welfare of oyster populations. The negative factors of the environment may decrease or inhibit reproductive capabilities, destroy the population by causing extreme adverse conditions such as increasing the incidence of disease, slowing the animal's growth and at the same time interfering with the development of its principal means of defense, the shell. On the positive side, the principal factors that favor the health, propagation and growth of the oyster beds, as the oyster community is commonly called, are the character of the bottom, the natural water movements, the salinity of the water, the water temperature and the abundance of proper food.

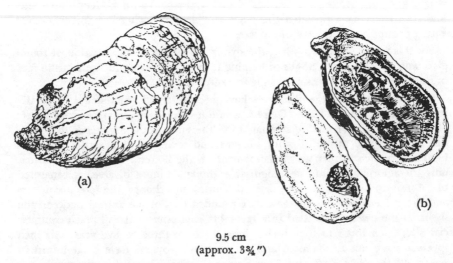

9.5 cm
(approx. 3¾")

Crassostrea virginica—The American Oyster. (a) Outside of the deeper left valve. (b) Left and right valves. The body of the oyster is seen in its normal position in the left valve.

Oysters grow equally well on a hard, rocky or shell-strewn bottom, on mud compacted sufficiently to support their weight and on a great variety of man-made underwater structures. They apparently thrive best where there is a free exchange of water; an ideal nonturbulent flow of water over the oyster bed is one that will carry away excreted material and feces, and at the same time provide oxygen and planktonic food. Since no *Crassostrea virginica* can survive several hours' exposure to below freezing temperatures, it does not grow near the surface in latitudes (such as ours) where in winter it may be killed at low tide or frozen in ice and carried away by tidal currents. Oysters are euryhaline organisms which means that they are able to live in seawater that ranges widely in salt content. However, when these animals live in parts of estuarine areas in which the salinity gets below ten parts per thousand, they may be seriously affected by fresh water; indeed, it has been shown experimentally by Victor Loosanoff that the reproductive capability of oysters can be seriously inhibited by such dilution. Unlike many other species of oysters, *Crassostrea virginica* can live in waters that range from 1° Centigrade to about 36° Centigrade, but exposure of oysters living intertidally or on shallow sand flats to longer than several hours of more extreme temperatures is often fatal. Being headless, oysters feed by filtering the water as it passes over their gills, retaining and passing toward their mouths selected microorganisms that become embedded in the mucous secreted and discharged by special cells. These cells are part of the ciliated tissue that covers the gills. The best environmental conditions for the feeding of *Crassostrea* apparently occur when pollution-free water containing a low concentration of small phytoplankters (diatoms and dinoflagellates) passes across these oysters at a reasonable speed in a nonturbulent flow.

Unique among fellow bivalves is the oyster's sex life. It is estimated that a single large oyster spawns as many as 60,000,000 eggs at a time; however, averaging edible oysters of all sizes, a conservative figure would be nearer 25,000,000. More interesting is the story of their sexual eccentricities. In brief, the American oyster starts essentially as a hermaphrodite, as a male, as a female, or undifferentiated and changes its sex repeatedly during its life. In the colder waters of New England, many oysters ordinarily change their sex once a year—and this during the warmer months; during the winter months they become neutral or inactive. To the zoologist this type of behavior is known as alternative sexuality.

At one time, not so very long ago, the oyster harvest in Rhode Island waters was valued at many tens of thousands of dollars. According to the *Fishery Statistics of the United States* in 1961 only 7,000 pounds of oysters from Rhode Island were marketed, bringing in $7,000, whereas during the same period in Connecticut 359,000 pounds brought in $416,000. A similar source of these statistics revealed that in 1970, the commercial catch in Rhode Island had gone down drastically to 146 pounds valued wholesale at $179.00. The decline in Rhode Island has been due largely to our disregard for the cleanliness and general housekeeping of both Narragansett Bay and Point Judith Pond. With good management and pollution abatement in these and other areas the disappearing oyster can once more become an asset to both our bank accounts and our dinner tables.

The verse from *The Detroit Free Press* prefacing this article illustrates a belief held until fairly recent times that oysters should be eaten only during the months of the year with an "R" in their names. The R-less months occur during summer. The idea behind this belief was fairly sound since temperature affects the life of the oyster by controlling the rate of water tranposrt and hence the feeding, respiration, gonad formation, and spawning of these animals. The period of maximal feeding and growth in *Crassostrea* is during the colder winter months, while the reproductive season is restricted to the summer months. This means that oysters are less fat and least desirable for eating, most full of reproductive products for continued replacement, and spoil quickest when removed from their environment during the R-less summer months. However, today with rapid transportation and modern refrigeration, spoilage and loss has been decreased to the point where it is safe to eat oysters in this part of the world year round—although gourmets to a man agree that they are not nearly as delicious as those collected during the cool seasons.

The Immigrant Snail

The edible periwinkle, *Littorina littorea,* belongs to a worldwide family of common, abundant gastropods or snails, found singly or more often in great groups on pilings, rocks, boulders, cobbles and similar substrata, not only between the tides, but often as far as the reach of splashing spray from incoming rollers. Those above the low tides are well able to withstand the periods between high tides, remaining as if glued to the rocks to which they have fastened.

Periwinkles are algae eaters and vary greatly in color; the full-grown one-inch adults may be olive, brown, yellow, pale orange, gray, or more rarely banded or entirely black. Although along this part of the New England coast it is the most common snail in its particular environment, it is not native to North America. Presumably it was brought to this coast accidentally on a ship's bottom around the turn of the century, and finding both shelter and food in abundance, became at once a prominent member of the North Atlantic coast community. One group of zoologists believes that it spread to the littoral North Atlantic coast of this country by slowly working its way to Iceland, then Greenland, and finally Canada before starting southward. In any case they are here, and they are delicious!

2 cm
(approx. ¾")

Littorina littorea—The Common Periwinkle.

They have been eaten roasted, stewed or boiled on the continent and particularly in England for hundreds of years. For the year 1867 it was estimated that the annual consumption of periwinkles in London was 76,000 baskets weighing 1900 tons and worth upwards of $50,000. That is a lot of snails! According to M. S. Lovell, Athenaeus in his *Deipnosophists* says: ". . . of the black and red kinds of periwinkles the larger are exceedingly palatable, especially those that are caught in the spring. As a general rule, all of them are good for the stomach, and digestible when eaten with cinnamon and pepper." Periwinkles may be collected at any time of the year, but are thought to be most flavorful from September to mid-March.

In Anglo-Saxon, the periwinkle is called "sea-snaegl" or sea snail; in Ireland, the "horse-winkle" and "shellimidy forragy," and at Belfast, "whelks;" in Cornwall, "gwean"; in France, "sabot" or wooden shoe, or "vignot," and "bigorneau"; and in Brittany "vrelin" or "brelin." It is interesting to note that the Chinese esteem these snails and make a sort of ragout of them. Evidence of their long popularity as an article of food along the European coast is provided by the tremendous numbers found in the Danish shell mounds and by the fact that they are the most abundant shell in similar human deposits in Scotland.

It is best to collect periwinkles in sacks or in buckets from unpolluted areas where a good current runs or where there is obvious tidal flow. They can be stored for a short time but be sure to cull the dead ones before cooking. They should never be eaten raw.

The Sharpest Clam of All

As one walks along the coastal beaches of the Atlantic at low tide on a beautiful summer day, treading the damp and sometimes compacted sand between the tide lines, it is difficult to realize that this apparently barren section of the intertidal beach is probably peopled by an unbelievably large number of sizeable animals. The bivalves, snails, worms and crustaceans are buried beneath the surface with scarcely a visible trace remaining except to the more practiced observer.

The mostly ill-defined tracks and trails will help find some of these animals, but for the many beasts who do not leave their burrows, one must be able to identify the makers by holes, tubes and channels that can be detected. The shapes and sizes of the excavated sediment associated with the holes are unique for most species, and the types and styles of the sometimes elaborately constructed tubes are characteristic for many forms. The most profitable method is to study the hole or tube, perhaps photograph it, and then excavate the animal.

The neophyte unfortunately will not find it easy to dig out a burrowing animal from an intertidal sand flat. He will find difficulty not with those near the surface, but with the beasts that either live in long tubes that go deep into the substratum or that can dig almost as fast as one can shovel. One of the latter group, and probably the fastest bivalve digger on our beaches is the common or northern razor clam, sometimes called the northern jackknife clam, *Ensis directus,* an animal that uses its lone muscular foot for digging. Its hole on the sand surface is small, elongated, more or less oval with slightly sloping sides near the entrance, and without any sand or castings piled around it. If the first or second shovelful does not expose the clam, one should try another spot since the animal may be somewhere in the wet sand that is pouring back into the original excavation.

The adult razor clam, from four to ten inches long and up to about 1¼ inches wide, depends on its burrowing speed for protection from the turmoil of washing waves. These animals can bury themselves completely in less than seven seconds.

According to the well-known English marine invertebrate authority, C. M. Yonge, "When the tide is in, the animals approach near enough to the surface for the short siphons to project above this, but when the water leaves the sand they retreat deeper, although their presence may be indicated by shallow depressions from which sudden jets of water and sand may be forced up by the animal. To be caught, they must be approached with caution, because razor-shells are highly sensitive to vibrations and at once retreat still deeper. A sudden dig with a spade or a tined fork may bring up an intact specimen, more often a broken portion. . . . A less exhausting mode of capture is to place a handful of table salt over the hole; as this dissolves, the increased salinity irritates the animal below and it may come to the surface and project the hinder end of the shell sufficiently for it to be seized and, with a sudden jerk, pulled out intact. Any hestitation will give the foot time to get a grip on the sand below and it may succeed in pulling the shell down or else the animal may be

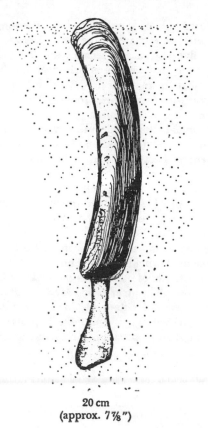

20 cm
(approx. 7⅞″)

Ensis directus—The Razor Clam. The clam's foot is extended as it pulls the animal into the sand beach.

literally torn in two between the opposing pull of hand above and foot below." This is because the thick, flattened, rectangular, arrow-shaped foot can be projected half the length of the shell, its tip expanded by being made turgid with blood to form a bulbous anchor in the sand, and its strong muscle rapidly contracted to pull the clam downwards. If the clam is carefully placed horizontally into the water, it will often leap forward by a kind of water-jet propulsion.

The common razor clam received its name because it resembles nothing so much as the handle of an old-fashioned straight razor. The sharp-edged basically white shells of living healthy specimens are most often covered by a relatively bright greenish-yellow thin layer (periostracum) with a long purplish area near the curving edge. Older razor clams and dead razor clam shells retain this coloration only in part and will bear the scars of abrasion as well as the appearance of abraded growth rings toward the more rounded end.

The internal anatomy and life history of the common razor clam is little different from that of other common lamellibranch pelecypods (bivalves) such as the steamer clam, quahog, cockle, and wood borer except for the already noted adaptations to its way of living. The posterior half is elongated, the umbones (original or earliest parts of the shell) are at the extreme anterior end. From this same end protrude the short siphons. They are united for about half their length. The dorsal side of the shell bearing the long external ligament is concave, and the ventral side convex. The ventral edges of the mantle (organ that encloses the bivalve viscera and secretes the shell) are entirely fused except for a small opening that lies posteriorly near the base of the siphons. It seems fairly obvious that its anatomical adaptations are closely connected with its unique habits. *Ensis directus* has been found in intertidal and subtidal sands from Labrador to the west coast of Florida.

A closely related animal, the fragile razor clam or the Atlantic razor clam, *Siliqua costata,* about as common as *Ensis* in our shallow water sandflats, but not as noticeable perhaps because of its smaller size (2 inches long by about ¾-inch wide) has a more restricted range, being found from Nova Scotia to Cape Hatteras. It has a thin, shining, elliptical, fragile shell that more often than not is covered by an iridescent periostracum that may lean to green or to purple. A white, fairly thick raised rib that extends from the umbo across the inner surface of each shell to the lower margin, often remains as a fragment on the beach, after the rest of the shell has been destroyed. This animal does not possess the remarkable burrowing habits of *Ensis*.

In my opinion, *Ensis* is one of our tastiest mollusks. It is excellent in chowder, and fried; it easily tops the steamer clam, *Mya arenaria*. As a matter of fact, razor clams may be prepared for the table in nearly as many ways as the common soft-shell and hard-shell clams. For those happily adventurous souls who wish to extend their gustatory pleasure, 1 recommend highly and without reservation the razor clam.

In Favor of Sea Slugs

The nudibranchs or sea slugs are oval marine snails varying from about half an inch to several inches in length. Adult slugs have no shells, for although a coiled shell occurs in the embryo, it is discarded soon after birth. These sea slugs are fantastically shaped and often amazingly and brilliantly colored; some of them are thought to be among the most beautiful animals of the sea. They are prime subjects for the amateur or professional photographer.

One may locate several of these handsome animals at nearly any time of the year in southern New England bays and salt ponds. They are found among the fuzzy white hydroids growing on fronds of kelp along the rocky outcrops, sliding through colonies of seasquirts that cling to pilings, or amid the ever-present sponges and moss animals. When one places any of the bottom species just mentioned in a large bowl or dish of seaweed, if sea slugs are present they will make themselves known within the next two hours by climbing the side of the container.

Nudibranchs are almost invariably found with the kind of food they eat, each species of sea slug remaining with the food to which it has become adapted. One of the adaptations that first captures the eye is that different species take on the color of the organisms on which they habitually feed. So it is that there are jet black, purple, blue, red, brown, orange, yellow and white sea slugs and they may be dotted, barred or striped. The texture of the animal's epidermis may vary too—from plain to warty or papillated. Combine these oddities with the sea slug's smooth, apparently effortless gliding either on the bottom, through the water or on the underside of the water surface film, and the results are striking.

Generally speaking, there are three categories of sea slugs, determined in part by the structure and appearance of their respiratory apparatus (nudi means naked, and branch means gill) which in all cases consists of exposed gills. The commonest type have a circular fringe of flattish tentacular or scalloped respiratory gills on the caudal (tail) end surrounding the anus. These are dorids or sea lemons. The aeolids or plumose sea slugs have the entire dorsal (upper) surface covered with long unadorned but colored pencil-like cerata or extensions of the digestive gland or liver. The third kind also has projections on the upper surface of its flattened, elongated tapering body, but they are branching and tree-like. In addition, the front margin of the third type has bushy and fringed bumps instead of tentacles.

All sea slugs have a pair of tentacles on the head. The aeolids in addition, have a second pair of somewhat similar thicker and twisted structures apparently adapted for smelling, called rhinophores. Some types of nudibranches have nematocysts or stinging cells borrowed from the hydroids (coelenterates) on which they feed. In several species, after the hydroid is ingested, its stinging cells migrate to the tips of the sea slug's cerata, and when the animal is threatened, the cerata are waved about, offering undischarged stinging cells to the trouble-causer. It is a unique phenomenon in the animal kingdom for one animal to prey on another, digest the prey's body except for its defense cells which are then used in turn by the predator virtually unchanged!

There are more than 50 species of nudibranches in Rhode Island waters and more are being discovered from year to year by interested malacologists. Some species are numerous only at certain times of the year when their presence may be detected readily by observing their long, beautiful and delicately coiled (usually white) egg ribbons. If carefully handled, the sea slugs may be kept alive for many months in a properly managed marine aquarium.

There is a related group of organisms known as sea hares that may be found in late August or early September in the lower part of either passage of Narragansett Bay embayments. These hermaphroditic animals may attain a foot in length and be several pounds in weight. They are washed into southern New England bays, often in large numbers, from warmer tropical Atlantic waters by eddies of the Gulf Stream. Sea hares are sea snails with two pairs of tentacles on the head, the back pair being larger and having some resemblance to the ears of a jack rabbit. In addition they have a transparent, soup-bowl-shaped, paper-thin shell covered by folds of the mantle and thus are, in a sense, a link between shelled snails and sea slugs.

The large brown and cream colored sea hares, sporadically occurring in these waters (genus *Aplysia*) ingest algae aided by their jaws and rows of backward pointing teeth (radula) and pass it into a series of three stomachs where it is ground still smaller by movements to a series of large horny teeth. When handled they may give off a beautiful purple dye which is thought to act as an escape cloud and to paralyze or somehow offend would-be predators.

Sea hares not only creep and glide like other snails but have broad lateral extensions of their feet (parapodia) large enough to enfold their dorsal surface completely. In some parts of the world, the parapodia are stewed or broiled and esteemed as delicacies.

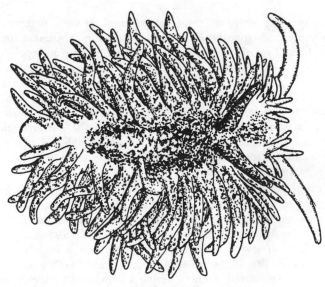

3 cm
(approx. 1¼ ")

Aeolidia papillosa—The Plumed Sea Slug (partially constricted) .

The Squid—Denizen of the Sea
And Delicacy for the Diner

The squid is a mollusk and belongs to a group called cephalopods, meaning head feet, that includes, in addition, different sorts of octopus, cuttlefish, sepias, the curly and paper argonauts, and the owner of the shell so valuable to collectors, the pearly nautilus. Squid are found most commonly off the New England coast in relatively shallow waters from 12 to around a hundred feet where they are caught in the nets of fishermen. During the spring months they come fairly close to low tide line along the shore where they deposit their eggs by the thousands in bunches of finger-like gelatinous capsules cemented to rocks or other types of hard substratum on the bottom.

It is difficult to see squid in their native habitat except by strong electric light at night when they may wander close to docks and wharfs. When observed in aquaria, their grace of form and movement, the large human-like eyes and the constant change of color that seems to glide along their bodies like passing shadows is quite striking.

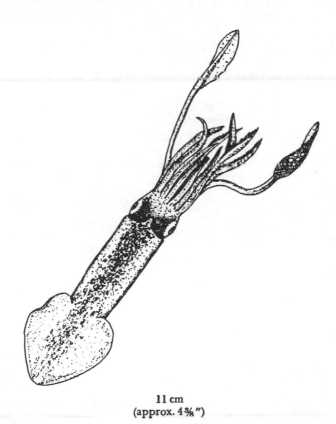

11 cm
(approx. 4⅜")

Ommastrephes illecebrosa—The Sea Arrow or The Flying Squid. Found from Cape Cod Bay northward.

Squid are streamlined and are able to swim faster backward than forward. This is managed by drawing water through a large opening surrounding the head and then forcing it through a small tube or funnel by muscular contraction of the body-covering or mantle. This is true hydraulic jet propulsion and by directing the funnel forward or backward the animal can progress in either direction. Its fins can be used for swimming but are more often used for maintaining its position. The ten tentacles or arms of a squid, originally mistakenly thought to be feet, extend from the head and are used in capturing food and in mating.

The only part of the hard shell of the squid indicating kinship with the mollusk, is a light, horny, transparent pen-shaped structure along the animal's back. This serves to stiffen the animal's body and support it. The squid thus becomes the only animal to furnish its own pen and ink. When alarmed, the ink sac expels a jet black ink through the funnel that clouds the water, hiding the squid at least temporarily from its enemies.

The local squid are small species from one to two feet long, but the so-called giant squid in the open ocean reach a length of over 66 feet and a weight of 42 tons. These giant invertebrates constitute a favorite diet of the great sperm whales.

Termites of the Sea

Wooden timbers and pilings riddled with contiguous holes are a common sight on older docks and wharves or washed up on beaches. These holes seem to have been bored by an experienced craftsman because of the apparent care and detail with which they have been made. The artisan is the so-called ship-worm, *Teredo navalis*, a highly specialized bivalve (mollusk) especially adapted for boring into wood. Shipworms are most closely related to the piddocks, animals known to shell collectors as wing shells or angel wings because of their snowy-white winglike valves (shells).

The valves of shipworms are reduced to two anterior vestigial (remnant) shells, about half an inch long and shaped like a double rasping organ, and to two tiny leaflike or paddle-shaped palets at the base of the siphons (two tubes providing for the intake and exit of water) that protect them from damage. The outer surface of each valve is sculptured with fine ridges with two rows of file-like teeth with which the shipworm scrapes the wood. The repeated alternating rhythmic contraction and relaxation of special muscles at 8 to 12 times a minute enables the animal to rasp off fine particles of wood. Although the wood fragments pass through the digestive tract, the shipworm apparently digests only some of the cellulose of the wood cuttings and converts it to sugar. The remainder is ejected, unchanged in composition, through the excurrent siphon.

The larger part of the animal's body is soft, lies outside the shell and may be up to 12 inches and more in length in a full-grown adult. It occupies the tunnel that it has excavated, and at the same time lined with calcareous or shell-like material.

Like many other sessile marine invertebrates (animals without backbones), the minute larvae of shipworms are motile and live for about three weeks as members of the zooplankton. At this time, if the larva is sufficiently fortunate to settle on a submerged timber it bores a minute hole just large enough to permit entrance of its body. This is only the beginning; it continues to bore, enlarging the hole as its body grows in length and diameter. Communication to the outside is maintained by a delicate pair of siphons, one pumping in sea water replete with oxygen and microscopic food, and the other pumping out the body wastes. The rate of boring is more rapid in young animals; a three-month-old individual bores about three-quarters of an inch per day.

Because the teredo, the most common local shipworm, never enlarges the entrance, of necessity it must remain in its burrow for life. In any case, it continues to tunnel with the grain of the wood, following the course of least resistance, turning aside for knots or for the burrows of neighboring shipworms. Since the entrance holes are minute, the damage produced by boring shipworms often goes undetected until the interior of the timber is completely destroyed and eventually the wood becomes so weakened by riddling teredos that it falls apart.

Sexual reproduction in the teredo is protandrous (all are males first) and W. R. Coe who studied their life history stated that "there is a graded series of ambisexual or hermaphroditic individuals." Ruth L. Turner pointed out the interesting fact that in the young there are two types of males, those which soon change to females and those which remain males for nearly the entire life of the animal. Fertilization in the Atlantic shipworms occurs after the sperm, shed into the seawater, are taken into the female through the incurrent siphon where they contact the small white eggs.

Because of their destructiveness to wharves, pilings, ships' hulls and wooden lobster traps, shipworms are often referred to as the "termites of the sea." Although they decimate much of man's marine construction and are thus economically important, they serve a useful purpose in the continuing cycle of sea elements by helping reduce the wood mechanically to its constituent parts. Interestingly enough, shipworms are authentically reported to be eaten as delicacies by Australian aborigines.

The shipworm has been known and dreaded since classical times; it is recorded as having riddled the planking of Greek triremes and Roman galleys. Later on it is known to have destroyed Sir Francis Drake's *Golden Hind* and in the 18th century, it seriously threatened the dykes of Holland. More recently, between 1914 and 1920, in San Francisco Bay, it caused damage estimated at ten million dollars to ferries, pilings and warehouses. The longevity of a piling may be increased considerably by creosoting. Copper sheathing works well for boats, but is impracticable for protecting pilings. During World War II, the study of marine boring mollusks benefited from a research program of the U.S. Navy that resulted in the production of anti-fouling paints and other materials that have provided increasing protection from these destructive animals.

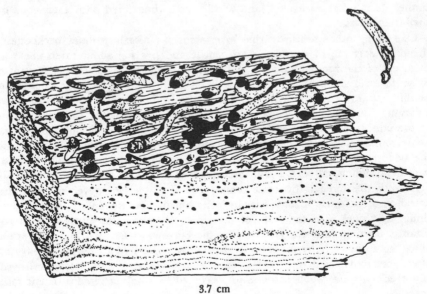

3.7 cm
(approx. 1½")

Teredo navalis—The Shipworm. A wormlike bivalve mollusk that does tremendous damage to chemically untreated wood docks and ships by burrowing long tunnels in the supporting timbers.

The Surf Clam,
New England's Largest Marine Bivalve

In the homes and offices of New Englanders who have regularly beachcombed the strands fronting the more exposed and sand-flattened, low sloping beaches, one often sees shells of the large and nearly triangular "surf calm" also called "hen clam" or "skimmer." The largest marine bivalve along this coast, *Spisula solidissima,* because of its size, and shape, provides shells that serve well for ashtrays, or as parts of handcrafted shell ornaments or beach montages.

Spisula occurs from Labrador to Cape Hatteras, North Carolina, and may reach dimensions of more than seven inches long by four-an-one-half inches wide. The inside of the shell is yellowish-white—dead-white after being repeatedly washed by tidal waters and bleached in the sun, and there is a large central beak covering a moderately sized spoon-shaped cavity. In this cavity is a dark-brown elastic cartilaginous mass that helps the shells to spring open when the muscles release.

As might be expected with a shell of these dimensions, this internal hinge, just below the membranes, is unusually strong. In living animals, the outside of the shell is either smooth or covered with concentric growth lines.

As the name implies, the surf clam lives in the surf, usually just seaward of the mean low water mark where it travels just below the surface of the sand. Here it burrows ahead with its strong, ivory-colored tongue-shaped or hatchet-like foot. Over the years, a unique method of collecting these animals has been developed: a wooden building lathe is sharpened on one end, and then at high tide is dragged and plunged into the bottom. If the sharpened end of the stick passes between the opened shells of a surf clam, the animal snaps together tightly, fastening onto the stick, and making it possible to pull the clam to the surface.

In general, clams and quahogs are relatively defenseless creatures that rely on hiding in the substratum for protection. The main enemies of this clam apparently are whelks and starfish. When one of these predators barely touches a surf clam, the latter is able virtually to leap out of the way by rapidly manipulating its foot. It does this by extending its flexible muscular foot between its shells, anchoring it in the sand and pulling the rest along after it. Herring gulls enjoy surf clams also, and in some areas the clams must be an important article in their diet, if one is to judge from the large number of cracked *Spisula* shells scattered on concrete roads and rocks throughout the length and breadth of the clam's distribution. The gulls pick up the clams in their claws and fly skyward about 100 feet, drop the clams and then swoop down to pick and swallow greedily the soft parts of the cracked mollusks.

Spisula is a fairly close relative of both *Mercenaria mercenaria,* the common quahog, and the larger offshore *Arctica islandica,* the black quahog, whose large populations and great economic potential were discovered in the early forties by Charles J. Fish, the first director of the then new Narragansett Marine Laboratory. Like these other two bivalves, the surf clam has an open circulatory system with a heart that should be excellent for physiological study: it is easy to reach, and can be readily perfused with various solutions whose effects on the rate of heart beat can be observed and recorded. Embryologists are also interested in *Spisula* because it possesses mature eggs and sperm late in the summer after most other local bivalves have finished spawning. At this time, the uniquely-colored, pinkish eggs and white sperm may be obtained easily from the ovaries and the testes respectively, of mature animals.

One reason that marine invertebrate ecologists have worked with *Spisula* concerns its feeding habits. In this animal, which feeds just above the surface of the bottom on material suspended in the surrounding water, the siphons are unusually short and their openings are strongly fringed. It has been observed that the tentacles around the incurrent siphon, the tube-shaped organ that carries water with its microscopic food particles into the body of the clam, readily act as an efficient filtering mechanism by keeping out materials unsuitable for the digestive system.

By local custom in some uninformed areas, people use surf clams only as fish bait, but it is easy to convert these animals into one of the most lucious shellfish table delicacies obtainable for the taking. After finding a good surf clam bed (usually sand pits and sand bars just submerged at mid-tide) one waits until the low tide that occurs a day or so after a full or new moon, and then proceeds to search and harvest the bed by hand.

If surf clams are included in clam bakes, only the young, smaller specimens should be used. Euell Gibbons, author of *Stalking the Blue-Eyed Scallop* advocates opening the clams with a thin round-ended knife, draining the bluish clam juice into a kettle to be drunk from a cup as clam "chocter" (nectar plus chowder!) made by heating it with an equal quantity of milk and seasoning with freshly ground black pepper. He then removes the abductor muscles, which he calls "beach scallops," rinses them in clam juice, and recommends eating them raw as they are, or chilled with either cocktail or melted butter sauce. They may be fried ᵥr made into a delicious clam chowder, and freeze well when placed in a container and covered with clam juice.

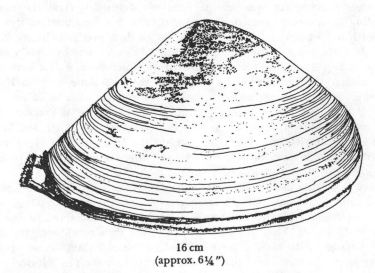

16 cm
(approx. 6¼")

Spisula solidissima—The Surf or Hen Clam.

The North Atlantic Coast's Largest Edible Snails

The best known whelks, or as the large species are sometimes locally called, conchs, to be found just below the low tide or in slightly deeper waters, are three in number. There is the waved whelk, *Buccinium undatum,* slightly more than three inches high that lives along the Atlantic coast from New Jersey to Greenland and also in Europe where it grows larger than it does here; the channeled whelk, *Busycon canaliculatum,* up to seven inches high, distributed from Cape Cod to Florida; and the largest snail growing in these waters, the knobbed whelk, *Busycon carica,* which commonly reaches a height of nine inches.

The waved whelk ordinarily lives on mussel beds where it can be found at dead low water, or it can be caught by tying a dead fish in a bag of cheesecloth and anchoring this bait among rocks near the low tide line. Its shell has six convex whorls, each with about 12 obliquely undulating ribs covered by fine spiral ridges or by prominent raised lines, a characteristic that gives this gastropod its common name. In the living animal, the outer covering of the shell is somewhat velvety, the shell opening (aperture) is usually lined with light yellow or white and the horny plate which closes the aperture (operculum), never seems to close entirely. The aperture characteristically has a wide notch at the lower side about as long as the spire and forms a short, wide canal. The body of the animal inside the shell is white, blotched and streaked with black.

The eggs of the waved whelk are laid in yellowish capsules, hundreds of eggs to a capsule, each about the size and shape of a garden pea. The egg capsules overlap each other and are sometimes laid in such numbers as to form a mass about the size of the palm of one's hand. In due course the young hatch and escape from the capsules as minute copies of their parents and rest on the bottom. It is said that sailors used these egg clusters to wash their hands and they became known in some quarters as "seawash balls." Empty balls may be found sometimes along high tide line still fastened to the stalk of algae around which they were originally deposited. If all of the young whelks have not escaped, the rattle produced by shaking the capsule briskly will reveal their presence. The waved whelk is usually carnivorous, living mostly on small bivalves and annelids (segmented round worms) ; it becomes the fisherman's anathema when it steals the bait from lobster pots and from cod lines.

The channeled whelk has a thin, yellow or fawn-colored shell, covered in life with a hairy periostracum (thin layer covering outside of shell). The outer lip of the shell is thin, the largest or body whorl (lowest whorl) is very prominent and carries along its outer edge a beading whose shape and size depend on the age of the animal. This whorl is prolonged below into a narrow, nearly straight, tubular canal. There is commonly a deep channel-like groove at the junction between the whorls of the shell. As might be expected in an animal of this size, the operculum is large; it is also rough and grayish-brown.

The egg case of this animal is familiar to many people because it is a common object on beaches at certain times of the year. It consists of a series of flattened membranous capsules almost the size of a half-dollar attached at one end of a tough cord-like structure. The eggs are laid in these upright edged, parchment-

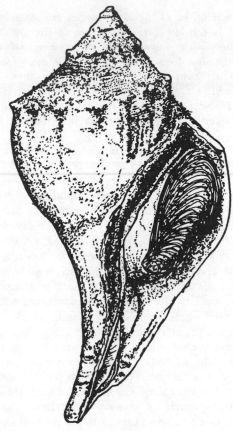

11 cm
(approx. 4⅜")

Busycon carica—The Knobbed Whelk or Knobby Conch.

like, disk-shaped capsules about an inch in diameter. The string may have as many as 100 capsules and may be over three feet long; sometimes it may curve on itself, and sometimes it may get washed far up on the beach and dry out before the young whelks can eat their way through. When this happens the shells of the young dead whelks will rattle if the string is shaken. This animal and its close relative, the knobbed whelk, are carnivorous, living mostly on other mollusks, worms, nemertines, and other likely prey. Both species are commonly sold in Italian fish markets, their feet forming the main ingredient of a delicious dish called scungili.

The knobbed whelk has a large, pear-shaped, heavy, ashen-colored shell that shows longitudinal streaks of brownish purple when the animal is young. The row of low knobs along the outer edge of the body whorl gives this species its common name. Unlike the channeled whelk, it has no periostracum, the ex-

100

panded body whorl forms an oval aperture with a long and open canal, the shell sutures are shallow, and the inside of the large opening varies from gleaming yellow to bright brick red. It is relatively common in certain areas in shallow water and very often living specimens are tossed or washed on the beaches by storm waves where the shell remains to be picked up by beach-combers after the animal has died and its soft parts have dried up and disappeared. The eggs of this species are laid in a similar manner and are essentially the same shape as those of the channeled whelk except that in this case the capsules are double-edged.

Both of these giant whelks or conchs have a large fleshy body with a broad foot on which they are able to move with surprising rapidity. As they glide, the shell is directed with the canal extended upward and forward so that the siphon protected within constantly projects its enclosed incurrent and excurrent tubes ahead of the animal. The head carrying a pair of stout, tapering tentacles with an eye at the lower outer edge of each tentacle, is beneath the siphon. A characteristically elephant-trunklike, constantly moving, long proboscis with a typical snail ribbon or rasping teeth inside the terminal mouth projects forward beneath the head. This apparatus is deadly for oysters and other bivalves. According to William Amos, the whelk grabs an oyster with its muscular foot, then whacks its own siphonal canal against the leading edge of the closed oyster. After the oyster shell is broken, the whelk inserts its canal into the break, and by twisting, cracks off enough of both oyster valves to thrust its proboscis inside and ingest the soft body of its victim. A variant of this method of invasion is for the whelk to grasp a clam or mussel with its foot and break its victim's shell with repeated heavy blows by its body whorl. These animals also use their ribbon of rasping file-like teeth (radula) to bore neat, round holes through the shells of a variety of mollusks before sucking out their contents.

Whelks and conchs are considered to be great delicacies not only up and down the coasts of Europe but also in the Bahamas and other islands of the West Indies where one can readily obtain in the local restaurants delicious conch chowder, conch salads and fried conchs.

Gastropods deserving great fame,
Call them whelks, conchs or snails,
  it's the same:
Their feet ground in a chopper
Or broiled with wine as a sopper
Will gain lasting gourmet acclaim!

Queen Quahog

Probably one of the two best known bivalves along the shallow protected salt waters of southern New England is the bivalve or pelecypod, *Mercenaria mercenaria*, (formerly *Venus mercenaria*), more commonly known as the quahog; quahog being the white man's attempt to pronounce the Indian name for this animal. Although it is found in sheltered bays and coves the length of the Atlantic Coast from the Gulf of St. Lawrence to the seaboard of Texas on the Gulf of Mexico, it is most abundant from Cape Cod southward.

It is of some interest to note that the scientific name of this animal, unlike that of many of its relatives, is reflected in the uses to which it has been put by man: *Mercenaria* is derived from the Latin word for "wages." It is thought that the great taxonomist, Carl Linnaeus, in giving the pelecypod this name took into consideration the fact that American Indians living along the coast, ground the shells of this animal into cylindrical beads from which they made "wampum" or Indian money. For this purpose, the often prominent purple area along the ventral margin inside the shells and near the muscle scars was particularly valuable; worth more than twice as much as the ordinary white kind made from whelkshells. Today with the resurgence of shell jewelry made from *Mercenaria*, these clams once more mean money to the many dealers in novelties whose stores are found in most of the vacation tours along the New England coast.

Mercenaria mercenaria is known by a variety of common names as quahog, chowder quahog, cherrystone, little neck, hardshell clam, clam, hard clam, and round clams, depending on political location and individual size. For example, in most New Jersey restaurants, a New Englander wishing to order *Mercenaria* would draw a look of amazement from the waiter by asking for quahogs, to get the food he wanted he would have to order clams or better, hard shell clams! Similarly, the smallest little necks and the next largest size, cherrystone, in Rhode Island are reversed in Connecticut where the smallest quahogs are cherrystones and the larger hard shell clams are little necks. In both states the largest size is the chowder quahog or "chowder" (used primarily for making chowder rather than being eaten raw).

By means of its powerful hatchet shaped foot, this animal burrows about on or just barely in mud, sandy or mixtures of these sediments on the flats, either just subtidally, or near the lower part of the intertidal area. The apparently ideal environment for growth of these animals occurs where brackish water resulting from the mixing of fresh and ocean waters, provides a reduced salinity that favors reproduction and growth, and at the same time serves to keep down populations of three of its most devastating predators: moon snails, oyster drills and starfish.

Over the years, a large percentage of the citizens of Massachusetts, Connecticut and Rhode Island have harvested quahogs either commercially or for private use. This has resulted in the development of a variety of ingenious methods for collecting these animals. Recreational shellfishermen who have become practiced in gathering hard shell clams have evolved what seems to be a "sixth sense" in gathering them; they may "tread" the bottom with their toes, bending down

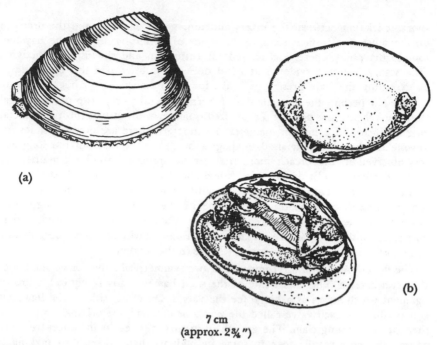

(a)

(b)

7 cm
(approx. 2¾")

Mercenaria mercenaria—The Hard-Shell Clam or Quahog. (a) External view showing valves, growth rings, siphons, and mantle. (b) Valves have been separated, body of the quahog is in the left valve.

to scoop out the hard shell clam by hand after it has been located; they may probe the sediment directly with their fingers in the most likely places until contact is made; they may use short handled thick tined clam rakes with or without a small wire basket attached to the head for catching the clams as they are scratched out; and they may have one of a number of differently shaped inner tube supported baskets secured to their waist to collect the quahogs as they are gathered. Commercial (licensed) quahoggers use far more efficient apparatus in working either individually from small boats or in crews on larger boats powered by inboard motors. The former may be divided into rakers and tongers depending on the type of gear that they use; the rakers use a so-called bull rake which is essentially a much larger and heavier version of the clam rake with the attached wire basket, while the tongers balance themselves at the gunwales of an anchored boat while working their 12 to 20 foot long, scissor-like wire-cap-metal-tooth-tipped tongs into the bottom. Rakers and tongers have to be physically strong and manually dextrous to work their unweildly collecting equipment and bring a sufficient number of quahogs into their boats to make their efforts profitable.

The dredgers work in deeper waters from 30 to 40 foot power boats specifically equipped with metal framed mesh bags (the so-called rockingchair dredge) that are lowered to the bottom, dragged for 15 to 30 minutes, brought aboard ship, and the contents spilled on deck for sorting by pulling the purse line. More sophisticated dredgers utilize a more effective hydraulic dredge that uses water jets to loosen the bottom in front of a dredge blade that can cut through the bottom to a roughly four-inch depth. Over the years there has been sporadic friction between the rakers and tongers on one side, and the dredgers on the other, the former accusing the latter of harmfully digging the bay bottom to the point where it is ruined for future fin and shellfish productivity, (the scanty scientific evidence at hand does not substantiate this claim), and of exceeding the state prescribed limits for the numbers of quahogs collected.

State law permits the amateur shell fisherman to take up to two pecks of legal sized hard shell clams per day. Legal sized quahogs will not pass through a metal ring an inch and a half in diameter. Fortunately, there are now stiff fines for anyone caught with undersized quahog, a misdemeanor that not too long ago was observed in the breach more than in the promise. Similar penalties are enforced against individuals taking these shellfish from habitats known to be polluted and so advertised. Increased pollution in several areas has resulted in the prohibition of harvesting from some of the best quahog growing areas; however, in the last two or three years, this situation is being reversed, and it may revert to the point where southern New England will once more become one of the best hard shell clam producing regions in the country.

The shell of *Mercenaria* is composed of two symmetrical halves or valves, hence the term bivalve. The dorsal side of the shell has an easily recognizable brown ligament which serves as a hinge for the valves. On either side of the ligament is a swelling on each valve called the umbo or umbone, the original part of the shell of the growing clam. The growth from this area results in concentric lines of growth, more readily seen in some individuals than others, thus making it easier to tell the age of these more conspicuously marked animals. The markings on the inside of the shell indicate the attachment of organs, the rounded scars being impressions of the various muscles that operate the foot, the siphons, and open and close the valves. The single distinct line connecting two of the larger scars marks the attachment of a thin sheet-like organ called the mantle, two of whose functions are to cover the soft parts and to secrete the shell.

Two edges of the mantle are thickened and fused one above the other forming a double tube, the incurrent and the excurrent siphons. The siphons are quite short and are darkly pigmented. Water entering through the incurrent siphon is drawn into a large cavity containing the two pairs of thin, membranous, folded, filamented (lamellar) gills. The gills have blood vessels and they are ciliated; the constantly beating hair-like cilia drawing a continuous current of water through the incurrent siphon into the gill or branchial chamber where respiratory oxygen is removed as well as the minute food particles which are in turn directed toward the mouth. Water bearing rejected materials and metabolic wastes leaves the animal through the excurrent siphon. The strength of the water currents is greatly influenced by the temperature of the environmental water, varying from greatest activity, at about 22°C, to cessation of ciliary currents below 5°C, when a sort of hibernation occurs.

The open circulatory system of *Mercenaria* consisting of an easily accesible three-chambered heart and connecting blood vessels has long been an excellent subject for study by physiologists and an equally good organ for research by students in this field. It is readily perfused by a variety of salts, drugs, and other solutions and the results of these experiments recorded with relatively little effort.

It is virtually impossible to differentiate externally between male and female quahogs. Each adult has either a pair of testes or a pair of ovaries which enlarge considerably during the breeding season. Spawning in this general area occurs from late June to early August when the water temperature has risen to about 70°F. An individual may spawn more than once in a single season. At this time millions of eggs and sperm are shed freely into the open water where fertilization takes place, (one female quahog was recorded as producing 24 million eggs at one spawning), the ensuing larval stages (trochophore and veliger) are rapidly completed, and the young minute quahog settles to the bottom in late summer attached to a sand grain or other particle by a self manufactured thread. Although, it may have buried at this time it eventually gets free, and following two years of growth, mostly during the warm summer months, it matures into legal collecting size by the third summer. Most of the larvae and minute young do not survive long enough to be collected, however this is not overly alarming since if even 1 percent of the fertilized eggs were to survive, the bottom would literally be paved with these bivalves! It is in great part the particular combination of environmental conditions at the locations where spawning and settling occur that provide for the success or lack of it in the size and quality of the quahog population. For this reason certain kinds of pollution are particularly harmful in the continual renewal of *Mercenaria* as a commercial resource.

There are two basic species of bivalves that may be mistaken for the solid, heart shaped, prominent beaked, 3 to 5 inch by 2 to 4 inch wide hard shell clam. One of them is a clam that is beautifully marked with zigzag lines of light brown on the shells and in lacking the purple border within. It is 3 to 4 inches long, is most abundant in the southern part of its range, has no common name, and is called *Mercenaria mercenaria notata*. The other is the so-called thin venus clam or widgeon, *Pitar morrhuana*, 2 inches by 1½ inches wide. It is dirty white with several rust colored or dark grey areas, the inside of the shell is bluish and it never has a purple spot. If ingested it will be found to be quite bitter.

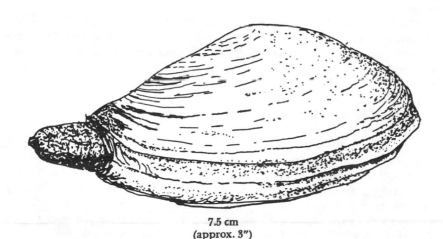

7.5 cm
(approx. 3")

Mya arenaria—The Soft-shell or Steamer Clam.

Orchestia, The Sand Dancer

". . . after prolonged examination of homologous
parts [of Amphipods] the observer would not be
so much impressed with the difficulty of a
common descent as with the intrinsic simplicity
of the processes by which these wonderful
differences of structure might have been produced. For if a son may be taller than his father,
a daughter stouter than her mother, in the same
family one child have straight hair and another
curls, one brother be smooth and the other a
hairy man, variations of a corresponding kind
suffice to explain the most striking dis-
similarities that the Amphipoda can furnish.
Lengthen or contract a limb, make a joint tumid
or flatten it out, multiply the spines or
prickles, narrow or expand the body, or so treat
one part of it at the expense of the other, let
it be cylindrical or depressed or laterally
pinched, stiffly outstretched or coiled into a
ball, — by such differences as these, in regard
to which many species present the most minute
transitions, it will be found that genera and
families are separated, without the least
necessity or reasonableness of attributing to
them other than a common origin."

Thomas R.R. Stebbing — 1888

On many of the cobble free strands of our shores, the observant beach stroller
walking down the beach slope towards the water, may find near the row of cast-
up seaweed that marks the high tide line, little openings in the dried sand
about 5 millimeters in diameter. Careful probing of these holes will reveal that
those not made by air escaping from the sand when it was last washed by a
flooding tide, will probably be the burrows of species of amphipods known col-
lectively as sand fleas.

The name, sand flea, or beach flea, is a good example of misleading nomen-
clature, the use of common names for ubiquitous animals. These marine beasts
are not fleas at all, fleas are insects. They are semiterrestrial crustaceans belonging to the Amphipoda (considered to be the most modern and the most recently evolved of the higher orders of crustacea), family *Talitridae,* (genera
Orchestia from the Greek meaning dancer) and *Talorchestia.* They are more
properly called sand hoppers. They feed, for the most part, on decaying seaweed and are harmless.

Sand hoppers are found most abundantly under piles of rotting seaweed left
high on the beach by preceding high tides, and it is in these long rows of
mixed species of dead and decaying algae that they get their food. After a night
of scavenging and feeding on dead plant and animal material cast ashore by
the tide, for which they will often make special trips from above high tide line
to the water's edge, the beach hopper excavates a burrow in the sand on the
dry upper beach. On the following night it will abandon this shelter, feed
again, and dig a new burrow.

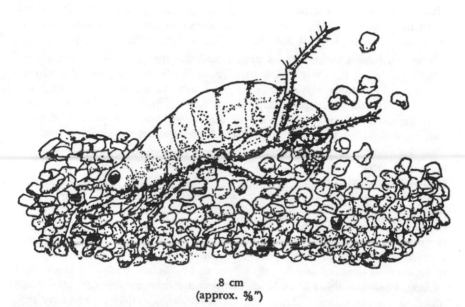

.8 cm
(approx. ⅜")

Orchestia agilis—The Sand Hopper, Sand Flea or Beach Flea. After a night of feeding on dead material thrown on the shore by the tide, the beach hopper excavates a burrow above the high tide line where it will spend the following day.

The burrows are built head-first. In constructing these temporary structures, *Orchestia* looks like a digging dog as it braces itself with its second and third pair of legs while the gnathopods push the sediment rearward to the back appendages and spiny tail fan, which spray it into the air. Final work on the burrow is accomplished by the utilization of a cementing secretion produced by small glands all over the body that enable the beach hopper to firm the burrow lining with sand.

Other amphipods live among the grasses and other flora of salt marshes, and relatives of *Orchestia* such as the side-swimmer, *Gammarus* (Greek for lobster), are abundant just below mean low water under stones, shells and similar substratal cover.

The body color of the beach hopper in resembling the substratum on which it rests most often, may be olive-brown or green to gray, white or translucent. Posteriorly, the animal may be bluish, while the antennae may range from red to red-brown. The animal is widely distributed along the entire Atlantic Coast of North America from the Bay of Fundy to Cape Hatteras, and is also found in coastal Europe. The body is strongly compressed from side to side. Part of the population of beach hoppers in a given area may be subtidal, if only during the dispersal of their young in the water column, a habit that can be used to advantage by a collector. In this case, tidal drift algae stacked at the high tide line can either be shaken over a clear spot on the beach and the animals picked up individually, or the seaweed can be dunked into a nearby tide pool, stimulating the *Orchestia* to swim out freely and climb up on the collector's legs from which they can be easily picked and put into a container. Preservation is best in a 5% formalin seawater mixture.

On occasion, the neophyte collector may have the sensation of being bitten when he picks up a beach hopper but close examination of the suspected bite site reveals, at most, nothing more than slightly reddened skin.

The appendages in amphipods have a basically similar structure and are arranged efficiently for their varied uses. In addition to two pairs of antennae anterior to (in front of) the mouth, there are the mandibles, maxillae and clawed prehensile gnathopods that help in feeding and in burrowing immediately posterior to (in back of) the mouth; then come five pairs of thoracic walking legs, to the first three pairs of which are attached the gills or respiratory organs; followed by three pairs of abdominal appendages adapted for swimming and three pairs of short, stiff appendages used as leaping organs. These animals swim infrequently, walking is effected by the walking legs, more rapid movement over the surface is accomplished by all the abdominal appendages, the animal leaning far over to one side while it sculls or darts rapidly over the sand, aided by strong, pushing strokes of the telson (tail). The characteristic vigorous jump of sand hoppers involves the sudden backward extension of abdomen and telson: a 2 cm. *Talorchestia* can spring forward more than 50 times its own length, a feat said to be unequaled by any animal its size. There are times when beach hoppers are numerous enough in a single place, to appear as small clouds when mechanical disturbance provokes them, and they all jump into the air at once.

In spite of their living out of water, beach fleas have kept their gills. However, because these structures compared with those of more aquatic amphipods like the closely related *Haustorius,* are reduced in size, the air must be humid for respiration to take place. This means that beach hoppers are restricted to inhabiting the moist sand that lies beneath the drifted seaweed, or that they must live in other similarly damp areas. The fact that beach hoppers react negatively to light and emerge to feed only at night is another adaptation that prevents them from dessication.

Little has been written about reproduction in beach hoppers. It is known that the males differ morphologically from the females, and further, that in the large number of species in the genus *Gammarus,* a related but aquatic form, the smaller females carry the larger males around on their backs for days before the molt that precedes the actual quick transfer of sperm. After this happens, the pair separates, and the eggs are released into the brood chamber on the underside of the body of the female and fertilized by the previously deposited sperm. There may be from 2 to 750 eggs in a single clutch, and several broods a year are possible. The young remain in the brood chamber (marsupium) until it is cast off by the female at the next molt. The freed young closely resemble their parents.

L. Pardi has described a very interesting experiment demonstrating a kind of 'compass sense' in the ability of these amphipods to use their eyes in ascertaining the sun's altitude, the plane of polarization of light in the sky and the moon's position together with some sort of internal 'clock,' to find their way to the level of the beach where they live. It has also been shown that under more natural conditions, for example, when removed from tidal wash and placed just above the water line, they can regain the locality high on the beach from which they came by quickly recognizing features of their original habitat, including the skyline, and then rapidly jumping toward it.

Thomas Roscoe Reed Stebbing (1834-1926) was the first man to work out many of the important subtleties in the systematics of amphipods, and his two major works (1888-1896) on the taxonomy of this group are still basic necessities for the specialist. Of these, his monograph on the amphipods collected during the voyage of the Challenger, the landmark expedition marking the start of Oceanography nearly 100 years ago, was his major work. According to E.L. Mills, "it stands as a monumental piece of scholarship and a major source of reference."

When the Tide is Out, Dinner is Served
"Outward Bound"

There are very few mollusks or crustaceans in the marine bays and ponds of New England that cannot be eaten. The vast majority of them are easily collected on pilings, between tides, in patches of eel grass, on mud or sand flats, covering submerged rocks and logs, or just below low tide line. Many of them are best eaten raw, all of them can be cooked, and in most instances the recipes can be interchanged without loss of flavor, texture or final appearance for the same kinds of animals. The table below indicates kinds of animals, their names, location, and methods of preparation.

Scientific Name	Common Name	Where Found	Method of Eating
Crassostrea virginica	Oyster	On hard objects in the shallows	Raw or cooked
Mercenaria mercenaria	Quahog	Sand-mud bottoms	Raw or cooked
Mya arenaria	Steamer Clam	Mud, mud-sand bottoms	Cooked
Crepidula fornicata	Decker (boat shell)	Stacked on hard objects	Raw
Natica, sp.	Moonshell	Intertidal sand flats	Cooked
Ensis directus	Razor Clam	Intertidal sand beaches	Cooked
Spisula solidissima	Surf Clam	Sand flats exposed at low tide	Cooked
Aequipecten irradians	Bay Scallop	In or near eel grass beds	Raw or cooked
Placopecten magellenicus	Sea Scallop	In deep water, off-shore	Cooked
Chaetopleura apiculata	Chiton	In shallow water on cobbles	Cooked
Cardium islandicum	Cockle	In deeper water, off-shore	Cooked
Mytilus edulis	Edible Mussel	In clusters on hard objects near low tide line	Cooked
Buccinium undatum	Conch or Whelk	Near low tide line in bays	Cooked
Littorina littorea	Periwinkle	Commonest snail on hard objects between and above tide lines	Cooked
Acmaea testitudinalis	Limpet	On rocks in shallow water	Cooked
Aplysia sp.	Sea Hare	On large algae in September	Cooked
Limulus polyphemus	King or Horsehoe Crab	Intertidal sloping sand beaches	Cooked
Cancer irroratus	Rock Crab	Among rocks and in sand	Cooked

Scientific Name	Common Name	Where Found	Method of Eating
Cancer borealis	Jonah Crab	Among rocks and in sand	Cooked
Callinectes sapidus	Blue Crab	Swimming in shallow ocean or brackish waters	Cooked
Ovalipes ocellatus	Lady Crab	On sandy intertidal beaches	Cooked
Libinia sp.	Spider Crab	Mud flats and oyster beds, etc.	Cooked
Carcinides meanas	Green Crab	Among rocks in shallow water	Cooked
Squilla empusa	Mantis or Ghost Shrimp	In shallow burrows in mud	Cooked
Many species	Shrimp or Prawn	Most easily netted in eel grass	Cooked
Homarus americanus	Lobster	In deeper water, rocky bottom	Cooked
Loligo paeliei	Squid	Swimming	Cooked
Arbacia punctulata	Sea Urchin	Low water to 120 fathoms	Eggs eaten raw
Strongylocentrotus drobachiensis	Green Urchin	Low water to 650 fathoms	Eggs eaten raw

By and large, collecting these delicacies offers little problem. One can walk along the shore with a bucket at low tide and simply pick up periwinkles, whelks, mussels, and an occasional oyster. Quahogs and steamer clams, enough for a single meal, may be dug in sand-mud flats as a family enterprise with shovel, clam rake, or plumber's helper. Crabs of all kinds, bay scallops and shrimp may be netted from a skiff or other small boat. A word passed along to friendly dredgers or fishermen may bring back sea urchins, crabs, mantis shrimp, deckers, and similar beasts. The only items on the list that may have to be purchased are squid (either fresh or freshly frozen) and lobsters. The best shrimping results from actively swishing a fine-meshed, long-handled dip net through beds of eel grass either on foot or from a sturdy skiff.

In answer to the many queries that are raised concerning the food values of these marine organisms, it is fair to say that all of those investigated have been shown to be generally superior in mineral, vitamin, and trace element content to what most people consider the more normal table fare. For example, it has been pointed out that weight for weight, the oyster is the most nutritious of all known natural foods.

Before using the recipes given for many of these animals, the reader may want to look over these general rules for their preparation. Perhaps the most important thing to remember is that all shellfish must be cleaned before anything else is done with them. Bivalves such as mussels and oysters, and univalves such as limpets and periwinkles, must be scrubbed under running cold water before they are opened. They may generally be opened by inserting a thin, sturdy sharp-bladed knife along a side away from the hinge and then working the knife around to the hinge, twisting in both directions in order to cut the muscles holding the shell together. Another method is to steam the animals in a deep pot in about an inch of water; they will open in a few minutes and the meats may then be removed for further preparation. If the shells of oysters and mussels have "beards" they should be taken off.

If limpets, periwinkles and whelks are to be eaten without additional attention, they should be washed and scrubbed in running cold water, then placed in a saucepan of cold water to soak for about ten minutes. Shake the pan until they all pull back into their shells, pour off the cold water and cover the animals with boiling, salted water. Boil them quickly for up to 20 minutes, remove from the shells and serve in white sauce with chopped parsley.

Crabs should be boiled in a saucepan in water seasoned with salt, pepper, parsley, and chopped onion. Add ½ cup vinegar, and 1 teaspoonful cayenne pepper to each 2 quarts of water. Put in the crabs and boil rapidly for 5 minutes, then simmer for 15 minutes more. When they are cool, remove claws and legs, cracking them with pliers or a hammer and take out the meat. Take off the part that folds under the body and at this junction insert a knife between the shells, at the same time twisting to separate them. The meat may then be removed.

Lobster should be placed in cold, salted water (1 tablespoon of salt to 1 quart of water) or sea water which is slowly brought to a strong boil. The animal may be removed from the pot and eaten at once, or it may be cooled and dissected in much the same way as a crab except that the tail should be removed from the body and the meat removed in one entire piece. The only parts of a lobster that should not be eaten, in addition to the shell, are the bag-like stomach and the featherlike gills. The pistachio-green, so-called liver, and brilliant red coral or ovary are delicacies and should not be discarded.

When eating shrimps and prawns the head and thorax (the part bearing the legs) may be torn or cut off, and the nearly transparent hard covering peeled off and discarded. The small black streak (intestine) may be removed if desired, but this is not really necessary. When using frozen shrimps or prawns do not thaw them until they are to be used.

Squid must be washed thoroughly in cold water, the head cut off and discarded and the outer membrane rubbed off and thrown away. For most recipes, a straight slit with a sharp knife is made the length of the body and both the cartilage or "pen" and the digestive tract are removed.

Sea urchins must also be washed, special care being taken to avoid being speared by the movable spines during this procedure. A pair of sharp scissors is then used to cut through the thin, solid but brittle shell at its widest circumference. The two resultant pieces are pulled gently apart. If the animal is a male (sexes are practically impossible to distinguish even by the most experienced marine biologist) the contents will be white or light gray in color and the animal is discarded. If it is a female a serpentine orange mass of minute eggs will be plainly visible. These may be scooped out and spread on melba toast.

In preparing seafood dishes avoid overwashing in running water, or overcooking to dryness. Remember that white wine is often an excellent substitute for water and that a sprinkling of fresh herbs before serving enhances most dishes.

"You must reflect carefully beforehand with whom you are to eat and drink, rather than what you are to eat and drink. For a dinner or meals without the company of a friend is like the life of a lion or a wolf."   Epicurus

CHITON

Chiton Soup

2 qts. washed chitons	1 potato
1 cup water	1 carrot
2 Tb. butter	1 garlic clove
1 onion	¼ cup celery
chopped parsley	½ cup white wine
salt and pepper to taste	buttered toast rounds

Put washed chitons into a kettle with water and steam covered for 10 minutes after the water starts boiling. Strain and save the broth. When the chitons are cool enough to handle, remove the meat and discard the shells.

Melt butter in a heavy frying pan or kettle. Add chiton meat, onion, potato, carrot, garlic clove, celery, all finely chopped, cover and saute until the onion is transparent but not browned. Combine enough water with the chiton broth to make 1 quart and add to the vegetables. Season with salt and freshly ground black pepper. Simmer 30 minutes, then add wine. Dish into bowls, sprinkle with chopped parsley and float a round of buttered toast on each serving.

CRAB

Crab Cocktail

2 cups crabmeat	2 Tb. horseradish
3 Tb. catsup	1 Tb. lemon juice
1 Tb. Worcestershire sauce	⅛ Tb. red pepper sauce

Mix catsup, horseradish, lemon juice, Worcestershire sauce and hot sauce and season with salt to taste. Chill thoroughly. Flake crabmeat and add. Serve in chilled cocktail glasses.

Crabmeat Omelette

3 Tb. butter	⅔ cup grated cheese
3 Tb. flour	1½ cups flaked crabmeat
1 cup milk	8 eggs
½ cup milk	salt and pepper to taste

Make cream sauce using butter, flour, 1 cup milk and cheese. Season to taste. Add crabmeat and keep hot. Beat together eggs, ½ cup milk and salt and pepper. Pour into heavy well buttered skillet; as mixture cooks lift it with broad knife to let raw part run below it. When browned, place in oven until well set. Pour a part of crabmeat sauce in the omelette, roll up, put on a hot platter, and pour the remaining sauce around it. Garnish and serve at once. Serves 8.

Deviled Crabs

meat of 12 cooked hard-shelled crabs

4 Tb. butter	½ tsp. horseradish
2 Tb. flour	1 tsp. salt
1 Tb. minced parsley	1 cup milk

2 tsp. lemon juice	2 hard-boiled eggs, minced
1 tsp. mustard	½ cup buttered crumbs

Remove meat from the hard-shelled crabs; reserve 6 of the upper shells and wash them thoroughly. Melt butter in a sauce pan, add flour, stir until smooth; add parsley, lemon juice, mustard, horseradish, salt and milk, stir until smooth and add crabmeat and minced eggs; Mix thoroughly, put into the crab shells. sprinkle with bread crumbs and bake in a hot oven for about 10 minutes.

Crab Supreme

4 Tb. shortening	2½ cups milk
6 Tb. flour	1⅓ cups fresh crabmeat
½ tsp. salt	⅓ cup chopped cooked celery
¼ tsp. paprika	⅔ cup browned small mushrooms

Melt shortening. Add flour. When the two are well blended add seasonings and milk. Cook slowly and stir constantly until thick and creamy. Add rest of the ingredients and heat thoroughly. Serve with mashed potato border.

Curried Crabmeat

1½ cups crabmeat	3 Tb. flour
2 Tb. butter	1 cup chicken broth (or other
1 tsp. finely chopped	good stock)
green onion	salt and pepper to taste
⅔ Tb. curry powder	

Cook onion in butter for three minutes. Add flour mixed with curry powder and chicken stock. Bring to boiling point and add crabmeat. Season to taste.

Crabmeat Salad

1 lb. fresh crabmeat	salt and pepper
1 heart of lettuce	mayonnaise
juice of one lemon	

Clean the lettuce and arrange 6 nests about four inches across. Mix crabmeat, lemon juice, seasoning as desired and enough mayonnaise to hold the crabmeat together when pressed into a small cup. Invert the contents of the cup into a lettuce nest and repeat. Put a spoonful of mayonnaise over each. Not over 1 cup (total) of chopped celery, apple, hard-boiled egg, olives, etc., may be mixed with the crabmeat if desired.

Fried Soft-Shelled Crabs

Use local blue crabs, green crabs, lady crabs or cancer crabs. Purge live crabs in a salt solution (1 tablespoon table salt to a quart of water) for a few minutes. Drain, dry and fry in deep fat until nicely browned. Serve on well buttered toast, with tartar or other sauce. The entire crab is edible.

OYSTER CRAB

Oyster Crab Newburg

Joe Cannon's column in the *Washington Post* (February 11, 1972) offered this recipe, serving four, for oyster crab Newburg. Mussel crabs would probably work equally well.

1 cup mushroom caps, coarsely chopped	1 Tb. flour
	salt, cayenne and nutmeg to taste
1 cup oyster crabs	2 egg yolks slightly beaten
⅓ cup sherry	1 Tb. brandy
4 Tb. (½ stick) butter	¾ cup heavy cream

Mix together the chopped mushroom caps, oyster crabs and sherry. Cover and let stand 1 hour. Melt butter in a saucepan. When it bubbles add sherry mixture and simmer 8 minutes. Stir in flour. Cook 2 minutes more. Season with salt, cayenne and nutmeg to taste. Add cream and heat through. Just before serving, stir in egg yolks, then brandy. Taste and adjust seasonings if necessary.

Mussel and oyster crabs can be sauteed in butter, or cooked in batter, or fried, and when they are served the latter way, they are said to rival the finest broiled soft-shell crabs. Pea crabs can also be cooked with the hosts and eaten together with them. However, the problem of gathering enough of these small delicacies limits their appearance on most dining tables.

CRAYFISH

Crayfish Salad

3 qts. large crayfish	1 Tb. onion juice
1½ Tb. gelatine	⅛ tsp. pepper
1 large can tomatoes or same amount of fresh peeled tomatoes	6 minced olives
	½ cup minced celery
juice of half lemon	1 minced green pepper
1 Tb. vinegar	1 Tb. prepared horseradish
1 Tb. Worcestershire sauce	salt to taste
	dash of cayenne

Cook the scrubbed crayfish five or six minutes in rapidly-boiling salted water to which a dash of cayenne has been added. Drain, cool, remove meat from tail, chop fine. Also take out black intestinal tract. Cook tomatoes to a pulp and press pulp through a sieve to make a pint of puree.

Soak gelatine in half a cup of cold water for 15 minutes, then pour over the hot tomato puree and add salt, lemon juice, vinegar and Worcestershire sauce, onion juice and minced pepper and a small amount of cayenne pepper.

Stir all together, cool. Set in refrigerator to partially congeal. Beat well, add all the other ingredients, mix vigorously, turn into a mold, dipped in cold water, and put in the refrigerator to set. Unmold, cut in thin slices, serve on shredded lettuce, topped with mayonnaise and garnished with large claws.

LOBSTER

According to Linz, Fuchs and Troup in their excellent cookbook, *The Lobster's Fine Kettle of Fish,* published by Citadel Press, two excellent lobster dishes are Lobster Cocktail with Cognac and Epicurean Lobster Newburg.

Lobster Cocktail with Cognac

2 cups chopped cooked
  lobster meat
1 Tb. chili sauce
2 tsp. lemon juice
1 tsp. minced fresh parsley

2 tsp. chopped chives
½ cup mayonnaise
2 Tb. cognac
salt and pepper to taste

Combine all the ingredients, folding lobster meat in last. Chill at least an hour and serve in cocktail dishes.

Epicurean Lobster Newburg

3 boiled 1½-pound lobsters
¼ cup butter
½ cup sherry
½ tsp. paprika

1½ cups light cream
4 egg yolks, well beaten
1 Tb. cognac

Remove meat from lobsters and cut into slices ¾ of an inch thick. Saute meat in butter 3 or 4 minutes. Add paprika and stir well. Add sherry and cook until wine has almost completely disappeared. Combine cream and egg yolks and stir slowly into lobster. Stir constantly until sauce is smooth and thick. Add cognac. Serve on hot buttered toast points, garnished with coral from the lobster.

MUSSELS

Fried Mussels

mussels
flour
garlic sauce or Hollandaise sauce

olive oil
salt and pepper

Scrub the mussels thoroughly. Wash in clear water. Place in a deep kettle without water and cover. Cook over high heat until the shells open (four to five minutes). Remove the meat from the shells, and roll in flour which has been seasoned with salt and pepper. Fry in olive oil until golden brown. Drain on absorbent paper and serve at once, with garlic or Hollandaise sauce.

Mussels with Tomatoes

mussels
tomatoes

bread crumbs
salt and pepper

Steam open the mussels, remove from the shells, and for each pound of mussel meat take 2 tomatoes, dice them and fry them in a little butter with a tablespoon of bread crumbs; season with salt and pepper. When done, add the mussels with a little liquor in which they were cooked, mix and serve hot.

Mussel Casserole

This surprisingly excellent recipe can be made precisely like an ordinary chicken and noodle casserole except that 1 pound of cleaned mussels is substituted for the chicken. If, after heating it for 40 minutes in a 350 degree oven, it becomes too dry, undiluted canned mushroom soup may be poured over it to remedy the situation.

Stuffed Mussels

3   dozen mussels
3   large onions, minced
1   cup olive oil
¾   cup long grain rice, washed and drained

1 tomato, peeled and minced
2 Tb. pine nuts
generous ½ tsp. of allspice
salt and pepper to taste

Scrub the outsides of the mussel shells. Rinse. Open with the point of a sharp knife, and remove any hair present. Rinse thoroughly. Loosen the joints so that the shells will remain closed after stuffing. Saute the minced onions in olive oil in a saucepan until transparent. Add the rest of the ingredients and mix thoroughly. When cool enough to handle, place a spoonful of stuffing into each shell (not too full, to allow for expansion of rice). Close the shells, and place in layers in a deep pan. Cover with a glass pie plate, and pour two cups of water over the plate. Cover the pan, and simmer over low heat for 1½ to 1¾ hours, or until the rice is cooked. Remove from pan and cool. Place in refrigerator to chill. Serve with lemon. Serves six.

OYSTERS

Roasted Oysters

oysters   melted butter

Many gourmets firmly believe that the next best way to eating oysters raw is to roast them on a grate over glowing coals. The oysters are scrubbed and placed side by side deep shell down on the grate. They may be eaten immediately after they have steamed themselves open, being spiked directly from the shell, dipped into parsley butter or brown butter and popped into the mouth. If they are permitted to cook a bit longer in their own juice, they are drier and assume an unbeatable smoky flavor.

Oyster Pan Roast on Toast

12 oysters shucked
1   Tb. butter
½   cup cream

1 Tb. sherry
Toast
parsley

Put oysters (1 serving) in saucepan and season with salt and pepper and butter. Cook over moderate heat until nicely poached. Add cream and sherry. Put oysters on toast, pour the broth over them and sprinkle with chopped parsley.

This can be varied by using 3 tablespoons Worcestershire sauce, dash of Tabasco and a tablespoon of chili sauce instead of the cream and sherry. It makes a hotter broth.

SHRIMP

Canape of Shrimp
anchovy butter
minced cooked shrimp
minced green pepper
minced apple

mayonnaise
thin slices tomato
chopped egg

Spread anchovy butter on toast cut into fancy shapes. Combine minced shrimp, red and green peppers, and some apple; blend together with a little mayonnaise; spread on thin slices of tomatoes, lay on toast, decorate with chopped eggs, bits of shrimp, and peppers.

Shrimp Cocktail
juice of ½ lemon
8 drops Tabasco sauce
1 can shrimp

½ tsp. vinegar
½ tsp. horseradish
½ tsp. tomato catsup

Mix together. Serve in thoroughly chilled glasses.

Creole Gumbo
1 chicken
1 onion, sliced
1 Tb. flour
2 dozen oysters
several pieces of ham

1½ qts. water
chopped parsley
salt
strong pepper
1 large can shrimp

Cut chicken in pieces and fry in hot lard. Add onion, flour, oysters and ham, and fry until brown. Add water and simmer for an hour. Season with parsley, salt and pepper. Add shrimp and cook for fifteen minutes longer; then pour at once into a tureen, and add boiled rice.

Shrimp in Blankets
shrimp
sliced bacon
quartered lemon

milk
salt and pepper
toasted wafers

Soak shrimp in milk, with seasoning, wrap them in thin slices of bacon; broil until brown on both sides. Serve on toasted wafers, with quartered lemons.

French-Fried Shrimp
1½ lbs. shrimp
2 Tb. melted butter
1 cup chopped green
   pepper

1 cup chopped onions
⅛ tsp. paprika
1 pint stewed tomato
salt and pepper

Peel shrimp, wash and remove sand vein. Cook onion, green pepper and garlic in the butter until pepper is tender, then add tomato and seasonings and cook over high heat 5 minutes. Add shrimp to this and cook 10 minutes longer.

SQUID

Squid in its Ink

6 small squid	½ cup boiling water
1 onion, chopped	1 cup cooked rice
2 garlic cloves, minced	2 tomatoes, chopped
½ cup olive oil	salt and pepper
minced parsley	

Clean and wash squid, reserving the ink sacs, and cut the bodies and tentacles into pieces. Saute onion and garlic in olive oil until the onion is lightly browned. Add the squid and boiling water and simmer for 15 minutes. Add rice, tomatoes, and the ink from the sacs and mix well. Cover and cook over a low flame for about 20 minutes, or until the squid is tender. The cooking time will depend on the size of the squid. Add salt and pepper to taste and sprinkle generously with parsley.

Squid Cacciatore Ranger Hall

12 small squid	¼-⅓ pint prepared
¼ clove garlic, minced	spaghetti sauce
⅓ lb. mushrooms, sliced	toast points
4 slices bread, crumbled	¾ tsp. salt
1 Tb. parsley, chopped	½ tsp. pepper
6 Tb. olive oil	¼ tsp. oregano

Clean, skin, and wash fresh or thawed fresh-frozen squid. Cut off the tentacles, remove the viscera, and discard. With a sharp knife, slice the bodies into strips an inch to an inch and a half wide and set aside. Mix garlic, mushroms, bread, parsley, salt, pepper, oregano and olive oil. Arrange around the center of a cast-iron skillet. Into the center of the skillet pour your favorite spaghetti meat sauce and turn the heat to low. Place the squid strips in the warm spaghetti meat sauce for about 5 minutes. Mix in other ingredients, turn heat up slightly and cook for 10 to 15 minutes, stirring occasionally until squid is white, slightly curled and tender. Serve on toast points. This recipe was developed and used by the class in invertebrate zoology at the University of Rhode Island.

Small Squid Genoa

3 lbs. small squid	½ lb. mushrooms, sliced
2 onions, chopped	½ tsp. rosemary
6 Tb. olive oil	4 Tb. tomato puree
2 Tb. minced parsley	1 cup water
1 clove garlic, minced	

Clean, skin, and wash squid and cut them into serving pieces. Saute onions in olive oil until they are lightly browned. Add parsley, garlic, mushrooms, and rosemary and cook for 5 minutes. Add the squid, tomato puree, and water, cover, and cook gently for about 40 minutes, or until the squid are tender.

Squid Sailor Style

4 squid
3 medium-sized onions
1 garlic clove
1 tsp. parsley
2 Tb. olive oil

½ cup dry bread crumbs
1 egg
½ cup sliced or chopped tomatoes
salt and pepper to taste

Wash squid and remove head and tentacles, reserving tentacles but do not cut body of fish open lengthwise. Boil for ½ hour in salted water. Chop onion, tentacles, garlic and parsley fine and saute in olive oil. Add this mixture to dry bread crumbs. Then add the egg and mix well. When fish are cooked, stuff with breadcrumb mixture. Simmer tomatoes for five minutes in a saucepan. Place stuffed squid in baking pan with a little olive oil in the bottom. Cover with cooked tomatoes and bake for about 15 minutes. Serves four.

Squid Piquant

3 lbs. small squid
2 cloves garlic
½ cup olive oil
1 hot pepper

2 Tb. breadcrumbs
2 Tb. butter
1 Tb. parsley, chopped

Clean, skin, and thoroughly wash squid. Saute garlic in olive oil until lightly browned. Add the squid, small hot pepper, and a sprinkling of salt and cook over a high flame for about 5 minutes or until the squid are tender. Discard the garlic and pepper, stir in bread crumbs, butter, and parsley, and cook, stirring for 2 minutes longer. Serve with lemon wedges.

SURF CLAM (MUSCLE)

A good recipe for baked "beach scallops" as the muscle of the surf clam is called, is to wash 1½ lbs. of them in clam juice, place them in a pan with ½ cup of dry white wine, ¼ Tb. salt, 1 Tb. minced onions, 4 drops Tabasco and a dash of cayenne pepper. Bring this to a boil, cover and simmer for 10 minutes. Drain and save one cup of the broth. In the same pan, melt fresh salted butter, blend in 3 Tb. of flour and then add the broth and ½ cup of heavy cream. Stir constantly, and after it is thickened, add 1 cup of grated sharp cheddar cheese, and then the "scallops." Put it all in a casserole and sprinkle the top with ½ cup of dark breadcrumbs, and bake at 400° for 10 minutes. Bon appetit!

PERIWINKLES, WHELKS, LIMPETS

Periwinkles and limpets may be boiled or steamed as indicated previously. They are boiled in their shells, extracted with pin or strong toothpick, and swallowed immediately either before or after being dipped in brown butter. Some hardy souls hammer the end of the winkle and suck the snail out of the other end. They may be fried after boiling, either in butter, bacon grease, or in the batter indicated above for mussels.

References

General References to the Invertebrates

Amos, W. H. 1966. The Life of the Seashore. McGraw-Hill Book Co. New York.

Barnes, R.D. 1968. Invertebrate zoology, 2nd ed. W.B. Saunders Company. Philadelphia.

Bayre, R. M. and H. B. Owre. 1968. The free-living lower invertebrates. The Macmillan Company. New York.

Brown, F. A., Jr. 1950. Selected invertebrate types. John Wiley and Sons, Inc. New York.

Buchsbaum, R. 1948. Animals without backbones. University of Chicago Press. Chicago.

Gosner, K. L. 1971. Guide to Identification of Marine and Estuarine Invertebrates: Cape Hatteras to the Bay of Fundy. Wiley-Interscience. New York.

Hardy, A. C. 1956. The open sea. Hougton Mifflin Company. Boston.

Hegner, R. W. and J. G. Engenmann. 1968. Invertebrate Zoology, 2nd ed. Macmillan Company. New York.

Hyman, L. H. 1940-67. The invertebrates. Vols. I-VI. McGraw-Hill Book Company. New York.

Meglitsch, P. A. 1972. Invertebrate Zoology, 2nd ed. Oxford University Press. New York.

Miner, R. W. 1950. The field book of sea shore life. G. P. Putnam's Sons. New York.

Pratt, H. S. 1945. Manual of the common invertebrate animals. P. Blakiston's Son & Company, Inc. New York.

Nicol, J. A. C. 1960. The biology of marine animals. Pitman Publishing Corporation. New York.

Yonge, C. M. 1949. The sea shore. William Collins Sons and Company, Ltd. London.

Specific References to the Marine Invertebrates of The North Atlantic Coastal Waters

Abbott, R. T. 1968. Seashells of North America. Golden Field Guide. Golden Press. New York.

Arndt, C. H. 1914. Some insects of the between tides zone. Proceedings of the Indiana Academy of Science 12: 323-333.

Barnes, R. D. and B. M. Barnes. 1954. The ecology of spiders of maritime drift lines. Ecology 35 (1): 25-35.

Campbell, R. 1961. Report on the shellfish survey of Block Island. R.I. Div. Fish and Game. Leaflet 5.

Clark, H. L. 1900. The synaptas of the New England Coast. Bull. U.S. Fish. Comm. 19 (Doc. 426): 21-31.

Coe, W. R. 1912. Echinoderms of Connecticut. Conn. State Geol. Natur. Hist. Surv. Bull.

———. 1943. Biology of the nemerteans of the Atlantic Coast of North America. Trans. Conn. Acad. Arts and Sci. 35: 129-328.

DeLaubenfels, M. W. 1949. The sponges of Woods Hole and adjacent waters. Bull. Mus. Comp. Zool., Harvard. 103 (1): 1-55.

Field, L. R. 1949. Sea anemones and corals of Beaufort, North Carolina. Bull. Duke Univ. Marine Sta. 5:1-39.

Fewkes, J. W. 1881. Studies of the jellyfish of Narragansett Bay. Bull. Mus. Comp. Zool., Harvard. 8: 141-182.

Fraser, C. M. 1944. Hydroids of the Atlantic Coast of North America. Univ. Toronto Press, Canada.

Galtsoff, P. S. 1964. The American Oyster *Crassostrea virginica* Gmelin. Fishery Bulletin of the U.S. Fish and Wildlife Society 80: 70-78.

Hargitt, C. W. 1914. Anthozoa of the Woods Hole Region. Bull. U.S. Bur. Fish. 32 (Doc. 788): 223-254.

Hartman, W. D. 1958. Natural history of the sponges of southern New England. Peabody Mus. Natur. Hist., Yale Bull. 12: 1-155.

Hyman, L. H. 1944. Marine turbellaria from the Atlantic Coast of North America. Amer. Mus. Novitates 1266: 1-15.

Jacobson, M. K. and W. K. Emerson. 1961. Shells of the New York City Area. Argonaut Books, Inc.

Kunkel, B. W. 1918. The arthrostraca of Connecticut. Conn. Geol. and Natur. Hist. Surv. 26: 1-261.

Marshall, N. S., A. B. Chenowith, S. Woodruff and R. L. Davis. 1960. Point Judith Pond Survey. URI, Narragansett Marine Laboratory Mimeo. Rep.

Morris, P. A. 1947. A field guide to the shells of our Atlantic and Gulf Coasts. Houghton Mifflin Company. Boston.

Nutting, C. C. 1899. The Hydroids of the Woods Hole Region. Bull. U.S. Bur. Fish. 19: 325-386.

Osburn, B. C. 1912. The bryozoa of the Woods Hole Region. Bull. U.S. Bur. Fish. 30: 205-266.

Pettibone, M. H. 1963. Marine polychaete worms of New England, Parts I and II. Bull. U.S. Nat. Mus. 227: 1-356.

Prudden, T. M. 1962. About Lobsters. Bond Wheelwright Co. Freeport, Me.

Robbins, S. F. 1968. At the edge of the tide: Squid. Narragansett Naturalist. June 9 (3): 42-43.

————. 1969. At the edge of the tide: Anurida, the tide pool insect. Narragansett Naturalist. Dec. 11 (1): 38-39.

————. 1969. At the edge of the tide: Trumpet worm. Narragansett Naturalist. Sept. 9 (4): 10-11.

————. 1970. At the edge of the tide: Sea squirts. Narragansett Naturalist. Mar. 11 (2): 38-40.

Schmidt, W. L. 1965. Crustaceans. University of Michigan Press. Ann Arbor.

Singletary, R. L. 1972. Tide pools, nature's marine aquaria. International Oceanographic Foundation 18 (1): 2-9.

Smith, R. I. ed. 1964. Keys to the marine invertebrates of the Woods Hole Region. Contrib. 11, Systematics-Ecology Program, M.B.L., Woods Hole, Mass.

Sullivan, E. W. 1909. Notes on the crabs found in Narragansett Bay. 39th Ann. Rep. R.I. Comm. Inland Fish.

Van Name, W. G. 1945. The North and South American Ascidians. Bull. Amer. Mus. Natur. Hist. 84: 1-476.

Wass, M. L. 1963. Check List of the Marine Invertebrates of Virginia. Spec. Sci. Rept. 24, Virginia Institute of Marine Science.

Wells, H. W., M. J. Wells, and I. E. Gray. 1960. Marine sponges of North Carolina. Journal of the Elisha Mitchell Scientific Society 76:200-245.

Whaley, Chester T. 1958. The vanishing oyster. Narragansett Naturalist. Fall, 1 (4): 104-105. (Charlestown Pond.)

Zinn, D. J. 1950. Tethys (Aplysia) Willcoxi in Narragansett Bay and other Rhode Island waters. The Nautilus 64 (2): 40-47.

————. 1965. A local snail that harbors bathers' itch. Narragansett Naturalist. Winter, 8 (1): 26-27.

Recipe References

Angier, B. 1970. Gourmet Cooking for Free. Stackpole Company. New York.

Boulenger, E. G. 1927. A Naturalist at the Dinner Table. Gerald Duckworth & Company Ltd. London.

Bolitho, H. 1960. The Glorious Oyster. Sidgwick & Jackson Ltd. London.

Fish and Seafoods Cookbook. 1971. Better Homes and Gardens Books, New York.

Gibbons, E. 1964. Stalking the Blue-Eyed Scallop. David McKay Company, Inc. New York.

Gourmet Magazine, 777 3rd Ave., New York City, 10017.

Gowanloch, J. N. 1933. Fishes and Fishing in Louisiana. State La. Dept. Conserv. Bull. 23. New Orleans.

Heaton, N. 1951. Shell Fish. Faber and Faber Ltd. London.

Hunt, P. 1962. Cape Cod Cookbook. Gramercy Publishing Company. New York.

Linz, M., S. Fuchs and L. Troup. 1958. The Lobster's Kettle of Fish. The Citadel Press Inc. New York.

Milaradovich, M. 1970. The Art of Fish Cookery. Doubleday & Company. Garden City, New York.

Miller, G. B. 1966. The Thousand Recipe Chinese Cookbook. Athenaeum Press. New York.

Tracy, M. 1965. The Shellfish Cookbook. Bobbs-Merrill Company. New York.

Index

Acalephae, 21
acorn (rock) barnacles, 8, 35, 36, 37
acorn worm, Hemichordata, 30, 32
Agassiz, Louis, 19, 35
ambergris, 9
American Indians, 102
American Museum of Natural History, 81
Amos, William, 101
Amphinera, 74
Amphipods, 106
Annelida, 8, 24, 27
Anomiidae, 77
arachnids, 62
arachinnelids, 29
argillites, 7
argonauts, 93
Aristotle, 19, 64, 69
Aristotle's Lantern, 69
arthropod, 38, 56
Athenaeus, 87

bamboo worm, *Clymenella*, 28
barnacles, 8, 35, 36, 37, 42, 62, 73
  Balanormorpha, 35
  Lepadomorpha, 35
  Verrocomorpha, 35
  acorn, 8, 35, 37
  ivory, 8
  rock, *Balanus balanoides*, 8, 35, 36, 37
bather's itch, *cercaria dermatitis*, 81
beach flea, 106, 108
beach hopper, 8, 107, 108
Beagle, HMS, 35
Bechê-de-Mer, 68
Berrill, N.J., 26
"bigorneau", 87
biotite, 7
bladder wrack, 7
blood-fluke, 81
blue crab, *Callinectes sapidus*, 38, 39, 40,
  44, 45, 51, 112
boat shell, *Crepidula fornicata*, 111
breakthrower, *Glycera*, 28
"brelin", 87
brittle star, 29, 34
brood chamber, 109
Buchsbaum, R., 22
Bugula, 47

cabochons, 7
Calvin, J., 25
capitellids, 28
cephalopods, 93
chelipeds (walking legs), 40
chemoreceptor, 76
cherrystone, 102

chersodromid flies, 8
chiton, *Chaëtopleura apiculata*, 74, 75, 76,
  111
  Circaria variglandis, 81
  Ischnochiton (large form), 75
  Katherinia (large form), 75
  "sea beef", 76
chowder quahog, 102
cirri, 27
Cirripedia, 35
clams
  Atlantic razor, *Siliqua costata*, 90
  paper, 48
  razor (northern jackknife), *Enis direc-
    tus*, 88, 89, 90, 111
  steamer, *Mya arenaria*, 30, 40, 89, 90,
    105, 111
  surf ("henclam" or "skimmer"), *Spisula
    solidissima*, 97, 98, 111
  venus (widgeon), *Pitar morrhuana*, 105
clam worm, *Nereis virens*, 8, 24, 25, 27, 28,
  79
  Neanthes virens, 24
cockle, *Cardium edule*, 34, 73, 77, 89, 111
cod, 70
Coe, W. R., 95
coelenterates, 9, 16, 18, 19, 21, 91
colloblasts, 22
comb jelly, *Pleurobrachia pileus*, 21, 22
conch, *Buccinium undatum*, 101, 111
conglomerates, 7
Continental Shelf, 7
coral, 16, 17, 21, 23
  soft, 23
  star, *Astrangia danae*, 16, 17
  stony (madrepores), 16
crabs, 8, 14, 40, 56, 62, 111, 112
  blue, *Callinectus sapidus*, 38, 39, 40, 44,
    45, 51, 112
  cancer, 40
  fiddler, *Uca pugnax*, 49, 50
  green, *Carcinides maenas*, 44, 45, 112
  hermit, *Pagurus pollicaris*, 29, 34, 41, 42,
    43, 51
  Jonah (northern), *Cancer borealis*, 46,
    112
  "king", 48
  lady, *Ovalipes ocellatus*, 40, 44, 112
  mole, *Hippa talpoida*, 51
  molted, 8
  mud, *Panopeus*, 45
  pea, *Pinnotheres maculatus*, 29, 48, 49
    Pinnixa Chaetopterana, 49
  rock, *Cancer irroratus*, 111
  spider, *Libinia dubia*, 47, 48, 70, 112
    Libinia emarginata, 47, 48, 70, 112

crawdads, 52
crayfish, 52, 56
Crustaceans, 14, 35, 38, 56, 73
ctenophores, *Beroe ovata*, 21, 22, 23
cuttlefish, 93

Darwin, Charles, 35, 37
Davenport, Demorest, 29
decapods, 38, 56
detritus, 7
Detroit Free Press, 83, 85
devil's-apron, 7
dove shell, 41
Drake, Francis, *Golden Hind*, 96
dredgers, 103, 104
Dromia, 14
dulse, 7

echinoderms, 9, 14, 29, 32, 63, 66, 69, 71
ectoprocts (moss animals), 8
eelgrass, *Zostera marina*, 7, 48
eelgrass flies, 8
egg cases, 8
egg purses, 8
Ellis, J., 19

fan worms, *Hydroides, Potamilla, Sabella, Serpula, Spirobis*, 28
feldspars, 7
fiddler crab, *Uca pugnax*, 49, 50
Fish, Charles J., 97
Fishery Statistics of the United States, 85
flatworms (Turbellaria), 30, 33, 34, 62
　Bdelloura candida, 33, 34, 62
　Heptoplana, 33
　Micropharynx, 34
　oyster "leech", 34
　Stylochus, 33
fluke, *Schistosoma*, 26, 81
Forbes, Edward, 68, 71
fringed worm, *Cirratulus*, 28

Galtsoff, Paul, 83
Gammarus, 107, 108
gastropods, 8, 34, 74, 80, 86
Gibbons, Euell, *Stalking the Blue-Eyed Scallop*, 98
gneisses, 7
gold-tooth (mason) worm, *Pectinaria gouldi*, 28, 29
gonangia, 18
Gonionemus murbachii, 19
gorgonia, 23
Gotto, R. V., 29
granites, 7
graphites, 7
green crab, *Carcinides maenas*, 44, 45, 112
greenheaded flies, 8
gribbles, 8
"gwean", 87

haddock, 70
hard clam, 102
hardshell clam, 102
Haustorius, 108
Hawks, Alfred L., 5
hermichordates, 32
hermit crab, *Pagurus pollicaris*, 29, 34, 41, 42, 43, 51
Herrick, F. H., *The Natural History of the American Lobster*, 53
herring gull, 97
Heteronereis, 26
Hincliffe, Malcolm, 81
Historia Animalium, 19
Holmes, Sherlock, 19
Holothuroideans, 66, 68
Holy Ghost shell, 65
horseshoe crab, *Limulus polyphemus*, 8, 33, 35, 60, 61, 62, 111
　xiphosura, 62
"horse-winkle", 87
Hydractinia, 42
hydroids, 8, 18, 42, 47, 91
hydroid phylum, 21
hydrozoan syphonophores, 19

Irish moss, 7
Ischnochiton, 75
isopod, *Idotea*, 34
ivory barnacles, 8

jellyfish, 9, 16, 18, 19, 20, 21
　arctic, 9, 19
　frilled, *Dactylometra quinquecirrha*, 9, 19, 20
　Gonionemus murbachii, 19
　Liriope scutigera, 19
　medusa, 16, 18
　oceanic, 19
　Pelagia cyanella, 19
　pink, *cyanea capillata*, 19, 20
　purple, *Periphylla hyacinthina*, 19
　sea-nettle, *Scyphozoa*, 19
　sea wasp, 19
　stalked, *Haliclystus auricula*, 9, 19
　"sting", 20
　white (moon), *Aurelia aurita*, 9, 19, 20
jingle shell, *Anomia aculeata*, 77, 79
　Anomia simplex, 77, 79
　Filibranchia, 77
Jonah crab (northern), *Cancer borealis*, 46, 112

Katherinia, 75
"king" crab, 48
kitten paw, 77

lady crab, *Ovalipes ocellatus*, 40, 44, 112
laminaria, 7
Lankester, E. Ray, 30

Leucosolenia, 12, 14
limpet, Acmaea testitudinalis, 111
    keyhole, 48
Linck, Johannes, 71
Linnaeus, Carl, 77, 102
Liriope scutigera, 19
little neck, 102
lobster, Homarus americanus, 38, 52, 53, 54, 55, 112
    "chicken", 55
    spiny, Panulirus argus, 53
Loosanoff, Victor, 84
Lovell, M. S. Deipnosophists, 87
lug worm, Arenicola, 24, 28

MacGinnitie, G. E. and N., 49
Mackie, G. O., 19
Malacostraca, 56
Marine Biological Laboratory, Woods Hole, Mass., 79
mason (gold-tooth) worm, Pectinania gouldi, 28, 29
McConnell, James V., 34
McIntosh, W. C., 30
medusa, 16, 18
mermaid's toenails, 77
mesopsammon, 10
microfauna, 10
microflora, 10
Mills, E. L., 109
Mola mola (ocean sunfish), 19
mole crab, Hippa talpoida, 51
mollusk, 8, 14, 35, 42, 73, 74, 76, 77, 95, 96, 97, 100, 101
molted crab, 8
Monograph on the Sub-Class Cirripedia, 1851-1854, 35
moonjelly, 9, 19, 20
moonshell, Natica, 111
moon snail, 8, 43, 102
moon stones, 7
mud crab, Panopeus, 45
mud snail, Ilyanassa obsoleta, 41, 80, 81
mussel, 48, 49, 60, 73, 77
    edible sea, Mytilus edulis, 82, 111
    horse, Modiolus modiolus, 34, 82, 87

Narragansett Marine Laboratory, University of Rhode Island, 53, 97
National Wildlife Federation, 6
nematocysts, 19
"nettles", Acalephae, 21
neuropodium, 24
notopodium, 24
nudibranchs, 14, 91

ocean sunfish (Mola mola), 19
octopus, 93
ornate worm, Amphitrite ornata, 28, 48

oscula, 14
oyster, Crassostrea virginica, 12, 34, 48, 73, 77, 83, 84, 85, 101, 111
    "Blue Points", 83
    "Cotuits", 83
    "saddlebacks", 83
oyster drill, 102
oyster "leech" (flatworm), 34

palmated kelp, 7
Panopeus, 45
parapodia, 24
parchment tube worm, Chaetopterus pergamentaceous, 28, 47, 48, 49
Pardi, L., 109
pea crab, Pinnotheres maculatus, 29, 48, 49
    Pinnixa chaetopterana, 49
peanut worm, Sipunculida, 30, 31
    Golfingia, 30
    Phascolosoma gouldi, 30
pearly nautilis, 93
Pelagia cyanella, 19
pelecypods, teredo, 8, 34, 48, 89, 102
periwinkles, Littorina littorea, 8, 41, 73, 86, 87, 111
    "sea-snaegl", "horse-winkle", "shelli-midy forragy", "whelks", "qwean", "sabot", "vignot", "bigorneau", "vrelin", "brelin", 87
Peyssonel, J. A., 19
phyllites, 7
phylum, 12
planula, 18
plumed worm, Diopatra cuprea, 27, 28
polychaetes, 24, 27, 29
    Glycera, 28
    Lumbrinereis, 28
    Nereis limbata, 28
    Ophelia, 28
polychaete annelids, 8
Polydora, 79
Polyplacophora, 74
Porifera, 12
Portuguese man-of-war, 8, 9, 16, 18, 19
prawns (shrimp), Natantia, Palaemonetes vulgaris, 58, 112
Precambrian, 12
proboscis worm, 30
psammon, 10

quahog, Mercenaria mercenaria, 60, 73, 89, 97, 102, 103, 104, 105, 111
    black, Arctica islandica, 97
    chowder quahog, 102
    cherrystone, 102
    little neck, 102
    hard clam, 102
    hardshell, 102, 103

round clam, 102
quartz, 7

rakers, 103, 104
rhinophores, 91
ribbon worms, (Nermertinea), *Cerebratulus lacteus, Lineus, Malacobdella, Oerstedia, Tetrastemma*, 30
Ricketts and Calvin, 25
rock (acorn) barnacles, *Balanus balanoides*, 8, 35, 36, 37
rock crab, *Cancer irroratus*, 111
rock weeds, 7, 70
round clam, 102
Russel-Hunter, W. D., 30

"sabot", 87
sand dollars, 63, 65, 69
  northern, *Echinarachnius parma*, 63, 65
  southern, *Mellita quinquiesperforata*, 63, 64
sand-colored collars, 8
sand flea (beach hopper), 8, 106
sand hopper, *Orchestia*, 8, 106, 107, 108
sargassum, 7
sandstones, 7
scaleworm
  Harmathöe, 28, 29
  Lepidonotus, 29
scallop, 73, 77, 78, 111
  bay, *Aequipecten irradians*, 77, 111
  beach, 98
  sea, *Placopecten magellenicus*, 111
Schistosoma, 81
Schmitt, Waldo, 37
sclerobasts, 14
Scypha, 12, 14
sea anemones, *Edwardsia leidyi*, 16, 23
sea arrow (Flying Squid), *Ommastraphes illecebrosa*, 93
"sea beef", 76
sea biscuit, 66
sea cucumber, *Thyone briareus*, 29, 63, 66, 67, 68
  Leptosynopta inhaerens, 66, 68
  Leptosynopta roseola, 66
  Stichopus, 68
seafan, 16, 18
sea glass, 7
sea gooseberries, *Pleurobrachia pileus*, 21, 22
sea hare, *Aplysia*, 92, 111
sea lettuce, *Ulva lactuca*, 7, 33, 70
sea lilies, 63, 69
sea nettle (Scyphozoa), 19
seapen, 16, 18
sea pork, 9
sea slug (plumed), *Aeolidia papillosa*, 14, 91, 92

"sea-snaegl", 87
sea squirt (protochordate), 9, 48, 53
sea turtle, 19
sea urchin, 9, 23, 29, 63, 66, 70
sea walnut, *Mnemiopsis leidyi*, 21, 23
"seawash balls", 99
seaweed (chersodromid) flies, 8
Sepias, 93
seed plant, 7
sericites, 7
"shellimidy forragy", 87
shipworm, *Teredo navalis*, 8, 34, 95, 96
shrimp, "pink", "brown", 56, 57, 58, 59, 112
  grass, *Hippolyte (Virbius) zostericola*, 58
  edible, *Peneus setiferus*, 59
  mantis (ghost), *Squilla empusa*, 112
  sand, *Crangon septemspinnous*, 58, 59
silicious spicules, 14
slipper shell, *Credidula plana*, 62, 78
snail, 7, 8, 41, 73, 74, 88
  moon, 8, 102
  mud, *Ilyanassa obsoleta*, 41, 80, 81
sperm whale, 94
spider crab, *Libinia dubia*, 47, 48, 70, 112
  Libinia emarginata, 47, 48, 70, 112
sponge (Porifera), 8, 12, 13, 14, 47, 70, 91
  bath, 14
  boring (Cliona), 12, 13
  bread-crumb, *Halichondria*, 13, 15
  dead man's finger, *Haliclona*, 8, 13
  elephant dung, *Suberites*, 12, 13
  glass, 14
  horny, 14
  red, *Microciona*, 13, 14
  sheepswool, 13
  vase, *Scypha coronata*, 13
sponge, seaweed, 7
squid, *Loligo pealiei*, 93, 94, 112
Star of Bethlehem, 65
starfish (sea star), *Asteria forbesi*, 23, 29, 37, 63, 67, 69, 70, 71, 72, 73, 97, 102
  northern, *Asteria vulgaris*, 71
Stebbing, Thomas, R. R., 38, 106, 109
Stunkard, Horace, 81
sunfish, *Mola mola*, 19

Talitridae (sand hopper), 106
Talorchestia (sand hopper), 106, 108
thalassopsammon, 10
thalassopsammophiles, 10
"tepang", 68
Thelenota, 68
Thoracica, 35
tongers, 103, 104
Tremblay, A., 19
trochophore, 105
turbellarian, *Micropharynx*, 34
Turner, Ruth L., 95

University of Michigan, 33, 34
urchin
    cake, 48
    green, *Strongylocentrotus drobachiensis*, 70, 112
    purple, *Arabacia punctulata*, 69, 70, 112
    sea, 9, 23, 29, 63, 66

velgiger, 105
venus clam (widgeon) , *Pitar morrhuana*, 105
venus girdle, *Cestus veneris*, 21
"vignot", 87
"vrelin", 87

"wampum", 102
whelk (conch) , 8, 41, 80, 87, 97, 99, 100, 101, 111
    dog, 41, 80
    channeled, *Busycon canaliculatum*, 99, 101
    knobbed, *Busycon carica*, 99, 100
    waved, *Buccinum undatum*, 99, 111
Wilson, H. V., 14
wood borer, 89
Worm Runner's Digest, 34
Worms
    acorn, Hermichordata, 30, 32
    bamboo, *Clymenella*, 28
    breakthrower, *Glycera*, 28
    clam, *Nereis virens*, 8, 24, 25, 26, 27, 28
    fan, *Hydroides, Potamilla, Sebella, Serpula, Spirobis*, 28

flat, 30, 33, 34, 62
    Bdelloura candida, 33, 34
    Heptoplana, 33
    Micropharynx, 34
    oyster "leech", 34
    Stylochus, 33
fringed, *Cirratulus*, 28
gold-tooth (mason) , *Pertinaria gouldi*, 28, 29
lug, *Arenicola*, 24, 28
ornate, *Amphitrite ornata*, 28, 48
parchment tube (marine) , *Chaetopterus*, 28, 48, 49
peanut, *Phascolosoma gouldi*, 30, 31
plumed, *Diopatra cuprea*, 27, 28
proboscis, 30
ribbon, (Nemertinea) , 30, 31
    Cerebratulus lacteus, 30, 31
    Lineus, 30
    Malacobdella, 30
    Oerstedia, 30
    Tetrastemma, 30
scale, *Harmathöe*, 29
    Lepedonotus, 29

Xiphosura, 62

Yonge, C. M., 88

zygote, 26
zooid, 9, 42
zooplankton, 17, 23, 26, 33, 35, 37, 48, 68, 83, 95